MY
TWENTY YEARS
OF A
MIRACLE MINISTRY

By ORAL ROBERTS

PREFACE

Recently I stayed in a motel for a week. Some beautiful flowers had been placed in my room, but I was not really aware of them until the day we left. One of my associates picked up the flowers and asked, "Aren't they beautiful?" I replied, "They certainly are but this is the first time I have *seen* them."

While I may not notice flowers, I *do see* people. Jesus Christ has given me a feeling for people. He has taken me into the arena of human suffering. He has given me an urge to identify with people — to feel their pain, to share their heartbreak and to know their needs and dilemmas. God has let me see my generation — the one to whom He commanded me to take His healing power. He has shown me that people are bound by sickness, fear, demons and sin.

I have sought to be filled with the Holy Spirit so I could minister effectively to the people. I have had to discipline myself to express compassion instead of sympathy, faith instead of fear and response instead of reaction. I have discovered that it is relatively safe to preach but it is rather risky to invade the citadel of Satanic power where people are held in bondage. However, God is faithful and His power has been present to heal. As I have ministered by the laying on of hands and prayer, the people have responded in faith. Thousands have received from God miracles of healing and deliverance.

This ministry is built on the truth that God is a good God! I believe that the Bible teaches that men are to have life and have it more abundantly; that needs exist to be met; and problems, to be solved. I have learned to approach God boldly, confidently and in faith.

I have had my back to the wall. I have faced situations when a miracle was the only answer. And, God has sent the needed miracle. At times, it seems that this ministry literally has been sustained on a manna of miracles.

I have found that this ministry never slows down — there is no stopping place! Today, in 1967, I face the greatest challenges and opportunities of my entire ministry.

In this book, I share with you, my partners and friends, some of my experiences of the last twenty years. There is only room to tell some of the miracles and a bit of the conflict and struggle that preceded them. I trust that the reading of this book will challenge you to expect a new miracle every day.

Los Angeles Crusade, 1951. Early in my ministry, God provided me with the finest gospel tent and equipment in America. My first tent was 90 x 210 feet, with a seating capacity of 3,000. However, in only a few months, we outgrew this tent and needed a larger one to accommodate the thousands who thronged the crusades.

CONTENTS

In 1950, we held a three-day crusade in Enid's Convention Hall, the place of our beginnings. We were told the Convention Hall had an average seating capacity of 2,800, but by the final night of the crusade there was over 4,000 in attendance. Every seat was occupied; hundreds were standing and hundreds, turned away. This was a record-breaking attendance for the Convention Hall, reported an official. An Enid pastor reported, "This was, without doubt, the greatest spiritual awakening Enid has ever known."

THE FORTIES
Beginnings of a Miracle

This ministry began with a miracle — a miracle of healing. It began with the audible voice of God saying, *Son, I am going to heal you and you are to take My healing power to your generation* — a command so incomprehensible that I listened in awe. This command would mean years of inward change and struggle, years of molding of my life.

When I was fifteen, I ran away from home. I was rebellious. I thought I had all the answers, and God didn't fit into my plans. I wanted to be a success, to make money and to be popular. Just one year later I was carried home, hemorrhaging from both lungs. I had tuberculosis and was not expected to live. My world came crashing down.

My parents prayed for me and believed that God would save my life, but I was totally disinterested in God. People who came to visit told me that it was God who had struck me down.

God always has someone to speak for Him. In this case, it was my mother. She said, "Son, God did not put tuberculosis on you. The Devil is trying to destroy your life."

Never before had I heard the Devil mentioned in connection with sickness. It had always been God who got the blame. Shortly after this my sister, Jewel, came to me. "Oral," she said, "God is going to heal you." "Is he?" I asked. "Yes," she replied. For the first time faith leaped in my heart and I felt a desire to accept Christ as my Savior.

Things began to happen. Flat on my back, I came to terms with God. I gave my life to Jesus Christ.

One day my oldest brother came and took me to a revival meeting in Ada, Oklahoma, where an evangelist was praying for the sick. On the way to the meeting, while I was lying on a mattress in the back seat of the car, God spoke to me. He said, *Son, I am going to heal you and you are to take My healing power to your generation.* God not only healed me in that meeting but also gave me direction for my life.

I could not understand the complete meaning of God's command. Twelve years were to pass before I would begin to understand. During this time I evangelized, pastored churches and attended college. My ministry became acceptable. Still I was restless and unhappy. Some of our church leaders thought that my restlessness was a sign of instability and they told me quite plainly I should settle down and be content, but they didn't feel "a fire shut up in their bones."

MY STRUGGLE FOR GOD'S POWER

In 1947, God began dealing with me in a mighty way while I was pastoring at Enid, Oklahoma. Several nights in a row I dreamed a dream that haunted me. Each time when I awoke I found myself sobbing. In this dream I saw the human race lost, sick, afraid, frustrated, tormented and oppressed. I heard their screams of fear and misery, their sobs, their wails of frustrations. What I saw and heard and felt tore me to pieces.

At this time I was also attending Phillips University. One day I was sitting in a sociology class. My professor had just made the statement that it was scientifically impossible for woman to have been made out of man's rib. I was sitting on the back row, waiting for someone to take issue with him. Not a voice was lifted. Suddenly from out of my spirit I heard God's voice again, *Son, don't be like other men. Don't be like other preachers. Be like My Son Jesus and heal the people as He healed them.*

Be like Jesus, and heal the people as He healed them. This sentence echoed in my heart.

God showed me there was only one source of original information about Jesus and that is the Bible. He impressed me to read the Gospels and Acts through three times during the next thirty days.

On my knees I read every word in these wonderful books, despite my church work and college studies. Many times my eyes would fill with tears and I would have to wait awhile before reading further. Sometimes Jesus would become so real to me that I would look up to see if He were in the room with me.

I achieved a harmony with Jesus while reading the four Gospels and the Book of Acts. What He had done during His earthly ministry and what I felt I should do in my ministry were one and the same — to preach the Gospel and to heal the sick. I wanted my ministry to be against the same four things His was against — sin, demons, disease and fear. I wanted my ministry to emphasize the same power that His did — the miracle-working power of faith in God.

I came to a point of no return. At the same time it caused me to realize I had to have a direct contact with God in order to have this ministry. I had to have a visitation from God. I knew it would be a struggle because I knew my nature. Only a miracle could bring about such a change.

I went to my little study in the church and lay down with my face on the floor. I told God I was going to settle it once and for all. He would have to give me His power or deny me. There was no middle ground. It was now or never.

I poured out my soul, like water, before the Lord. Time merged with eternity. Slowly, almost imperceptibly, God began to take control of me. Suddenly I knew God was in the room with me. His hands were upon me and His power was coming into me. The old Oral Roberts began to fade as God took control. My struggling ceased. As I lay on the floor, God spoke, *Get on your feet!*

I rose up. He said, *Go get in your car.*

I got into the car. He said, *Drive one block and turn right.*

When I reached the end of the block and started to turn right, God said, *From this hour you will heal the sick and cast out devils by My power!*

The church I pastored in Enid. I had been here only a year when I answered God's call to this ministry of deliverance that has circled the world and reached people in all walks of life.

I PROVE GOD'S CALL

I decided to prove to myself that God had truly spoken. I secured the use of an auditorium in the Educational Building in downtown Enid for 2 p.m. the following Sunday and announced a service and invited the sick to come for prayer. I asked the Lord for three things: first, to give me an audience of 1,000 people (I had been preaching to a congregation of 200); second, to supply the financial needs in an honorable way; and third, to heal the people by divine power so conclusively that they, as well as I, would know I was called of God for this special ministry.

I promised God, *If You will grant these three things, I will resign my pastorate and enter immediately into evangelistic crusades.*

As I looked forward to this critical meeting, I was suddenly faced with an overwhelming sense of failure. I awakened one night in a cold sweat. I had been dreaming of standing before the people and having them pass by me in the prayer line. In my dream many outstanding miracles of healing had been wrought, but I awakened with the realization that it would be more difficult to get people healed in actual practice.

I slept very little the rest of the night. The next morning I awoke with the haunting question: *What if I fail?*

For two days I wrestled with this awful question. It pounded in my breast. *What if I fail? What if I fail?* Suddenly, very clearly, God said: *You have already done that.*

I was shocked to the depths of my spirit. Then slowly I realized what He meant. My mediocre preaching, my following the pattern of other preachers whose visions were limited—this was failure in God's sight, when compared to the ministry I should have had. When God gently pointed out my failure, He also gave me the finest opportunity I have ever faced—I could start over! A deep peace settled over me.

When I arrived at the auditorium Sunday afternoon, the custodian met me and said 1,200 people were present already. I wanted to shout right then and there.

Fleece number one was answered!

The service started and later the offering was received. I asked the ushers to count it and bring me the amount. The head usher handed me a slip of paper on which was written $163.03.

For the second time, I wanted to shout for joy. God had given us the full amount to cover all expenses with $3.03 over! Fleece number two was answered. There was one more to go—the healing of the people.

I read my text from Acts 10:38: *How God anointed Jesus of Nazareth with the Holy Ghost and with power: who went about doing good, and healing all that were oppressed of the devil; for God was with him.*

My sermon was entitled, *If You Need Healing, Do These Things.*

I was so overjoyed with God's answer to the first two parts of my fleece that my enthusiasm was contagious. Someone later described what happened:

"Brother Roberts was preaching when all of a sudden his face began to shine. He grabbed the microphone and ran a few steps on the platform. Without another word, he put the microphone down and leaped off the high platform. In that split second the crowd rose simultaneously and ran to meet him.

"The first person Brother Roberts prayed for was an elderly German woman who had had a crippled hand for 38 years. She threw up her hand and began moving it about, crying at the top of her voice, 'God has healed me!'"

I was so filled with the power of the Almighty that I seemed to have supernatural strength. It was nearly six o'clock when I finished praying for the last one who needed deliverance. When I left, there was not a doubt that God had called me and was with me for whatever the future would hold. Not only had many been wonderfully healed, but also more people came to Christ than I had seen saved in the past nine months of pastoral ministry.

That day there came a knowing within me—a knowing of God's will and purpose for my life. I knew I was called of God to minister His healing to my generation; I was born for this cause.

WE STEP OUT ON FAITH

Evelyn and I resigned our church and moved our little family to Tulsa to launch a world-wide ministry. "With what?" you may ask. With faith. There is no difference, I have discovered, between faith and knowing, they are one and the same.

Only a few people in Tulsa knew us. Steve Pringle, a Tulsa pastor, had felt led of the Lord to erect a tent near his church on North Main and to conduct a continuous revival for the summer. He asked me to speak for him on a Tuesday night. It was unseasonably cold and rainy and only about 200 people were present. However, a large number was saved. The healing power of the Lord was present and several miracles took place.

Steve asked me to stay and preach until Sunday. Neither of us anticipated that the crowds would increase until there would be standing room only or that the revival would continue for nearly nine weeks. Little did I dream that this was the beginning of a ministry that would move throughout the world.

MY LIFE IS THREATENED

One night during this meeting, bullets from the revolver of an enraged bystander tore into the canvas about two feet above my head and nearly ended my ministry. The story of this attempt on my life was carried nationwide by the Associated Press and it focused the attention of thousands upon what God was doing on North Main Street in Tulsa. Overnight, I was labeled a controversial evangelist.

The man who did the shooting was arrested and he told the police, "I don't know why I did it." His action was unlike the planned and organized persecution that I was to face again and again. When I was in the midst of severe persecution in Australia, I remembered this incident. It was an omen, and I am sure God was trying to show me that life is composed of positives and negatives and that they are often locked in deadly combat.

Buying this house was one of the narrowest escapes my faith ever had. I made the entire deal with only $25.00 to my name, but the Lord saw me through. My worldwide deliverance ministry had its humble beginning in this little house.

The first issue of Healing Waters Magazine was published in November 1947. It contained 8 pages — quite a contrast with the Abundant Life Magazine of today.

OUR FAITH IS TESTED

From Tulsa, I went to Chanute, Kansas. I was full of confidence, but there we plumbed both the depths and the heights. I expected the services to be a continuation of the revival in Tulsa. Although the people were respectful and attentive, they did not respond. Very few accepted Christ or were healed. By the end of the first week we had not received enough funds to meet our budget.

God used the healing of a blind man to turn the tide. As I laid hands on this blind man and started to pray, he threw off my hands and commanded loudly, "Take your hands off me. I don't believe God heals today." I recoiled as if I had been struck. The crowd saw and heard everything. With all the control I had, I asked, "Sir, why are you here? You know that I pray for people to be healed."

In an angry voice he replied, "My neighbors talked me into it, but I sure don't have any faith."

Standing there before the audience and the blind man, I felt a wave of helplessness roll over me. Apparently I was not to be given an opportunity to pray for the man. He had taken care of that. The thought raced through my mind, *Lord, have you brought this ministry this far to see it destroyed in a single crusade, in one night? Isn't there anything I can do?*

Gently the Lord answered, "You can love this man." Kindly, I said to the man, "God bless you, Sir. This is a free country. You don't have to accept my prayers if you don't want them. I love you and I am only trying to help." I felt God's Spirit then and I am sure that he did too for he said in a different tone, "Go ahead and pray for me if you want."

I touched the sightless eyes, asked God to open them and to bless the man. Everyone in the building watched him go, as his friends led him away.

Early the next morning the chairman of the crusade knocked loudly on my door. He had important news. "You remember the blind man in the line last night?" he asked.

"He was not able to sleep any during the night. Just before daybreak, he repented and asked God to forgive him. When the sun came up, he walked out on the porch and suddenly realized he could see the sun. He could see the sky. He could see the neighbor's house. As his sight became clearer, he ran across the street and began awaking the neighbors to tell them he could see. His sight continues to improve and he says to tell you he will be in the service tonight!"

That night there was an electric atmosphere in the service. The news had spread about the man's receiving his sight and God was using it to change the spirit of the crusade. A large number of people came forward to accept Christ, and in the prayer line there was an air of expectancy.

Near the end of the prayer line I asked, "Is the gentleman here who was prayed for last night, the one who was blind? If so, will you come forward?"

As he came, the audience broke into spontaneous applause. Standing there, he told how he had been unable to sleep for thinking about his life and how he had never really known the Lord. Remembering what he had said and done before me, he became ashamed. As dawn came, he felt a change coming over him. He saw the sun come up and realized his sight was returning.

I asked him how well he could see. "I am able to distinguish people now," he answered. "I can see you. I can see people in the audience, and my sight is improving by the hour."

His testimony became the force around which the Lord changed the tide of the crusade.

The people also responded financially. The budget was raised; and on the closing day, we had our largest crowd and the largest number of souls saved.

The Chanute Crusade was a test of my faith, but it gave me a deeper insight into the problems of people and showed me my need for more faith. Several times I had almost quit, but Evelyn talked me out of it. I am glad we held on to see God perform a miracle that changed the situation and brought victory.

THE POINT OF CONTACT

Shortly after moving to Tulsa, I conducted a one-night service in Nowata, a little town in northeastern Oklahoma.

It was in the prayer line that night that God spoke to me again. What He said to me this time helped fill another missing link between this ministry and the people.

I started to put my hands upon a little child's head and pray for him when I heard the voice of God as though He were standing beside me. He said, *Son, you have been faithful up to this hour, and now you will feel My presence in your right hand. Through My presence, you will be able to detect the presence of demons. You will know their number and name; and through My power, they will be cast out.*

Then He told me I was to feel His presence in this manner as a "point of contact," and through it the people and I would be able to release our faith for His healing power.

I have no idea how long I stood there with my hands stretched out toward the child. It must have been several moments, because I remember the thought that went through my mind: *The point of contact ... something you do, and when you do it, you release your faith ... this is the thing that I have been needing.*

When I placed my two hands upon the child's ears, I was immediately aware of a feeling of God's presence in the right hand but scarcely any in the left. There was a distinct difference. After prayer, the boy heard clearly and spoke distinctly.

At first I thought that everyone I prayed for would be healed if I felt God's presence in my hand. I soon found that this was not true. It was then that I understood I must always carefully explain to the people the value of the use of the point of contact and that they must release their faith.

Fremont Tabernacle, Minneapolis, Minnesota. Pastor Russell H. Olson reported this meeting in our 1948 Healing Waters Magazine. In part he said, "Fremont Tabernacle has enjoyed the most glorious revival in its history under the dynamic Holy-Ghost ministry of the Reverend Oral Roberts. In 17 services more than 390 joined the salvation line to be born again, in addition to the scores who received the baptism with the Holy Spirit.

"We in Minneapolis have never seen anything like this . . . we are thrilled beyond words to see and hear the wonderful works of God. People came from as many as eight states . . . and went home healed. . . ."

One of my earliest crusades was held in the Masonic Auditorium in Muskogee, Oklahoma. The auditorium overflowed with people. Hundreds were saved and healed. Pictured with her parents and me is a little girl who was a polio victim. She was wonderfully and completely healed. Today, she is married, has a family and still lives in Muskogee. Even yet, she is known by many as the little girl who was healed in the Oral Roberts Crusade in Muskogee. An up-to-date version of her testimony is in the March 1965 issue of Abundant Life Magazine.

WE PURCHASE OUR FIRST CANVAS CATHEDRAL

Through the first half of 1948 I conducted crusades in large local churches or in auditoriums where I was sponsored by individual groups of churches.

I soon saw that this course would not succeed. I had felt led of the Lord to launch into city-wide crusades sponsored by groups of churches. I wanted a tent because many people with real needs would not come to a denominational church, but would come if we were in a neutral place of worship. The canvas cathedral would provide a place where people of all churches would be welcome. This would remove the emphasis from any denomination and put it upon Jesus Christ. Also, many cities then did not have suitable auditoriums.

Surprisingly, this has not been a hindrance to people's joining the sponsoring churches as a result of finding Christ in our crusades. Notable examples of this are the Reverend Hansel Vibbert in Evansville, Indiana, and the Reverend James Hamill of Memphis, Tennessee, who received scores of new people from our crusades in their cities even though there were many other sponsoring churches. When the pastor is wide awake, full of the Holy Spirit and faith, he often makes many gains in his church membership through participation in the crusades.

I contracted for the first tent by faith with no money in hand. During the next several months, I asked 100 people in each place I ministered to give $10 each toward the tent and to share with me in the winning of souls. God quickened their hearts and in each place exactly 100 accepted the challenge. But I still lacked $9,000. Time was running out if we were to have the tent ready by June to use in Durham, North Carolina.

I went to a bank in Tulsa and asked them straight-forwardly to lend me the $9,000. The banker was in sympathy with my undertaking but said he could not approve the loan for such purposes. However, he agreed to present it to the board of directors. When I returned, he said, "I should have my head examined, but you have your loan." This was another evidence to me that I was following God's plan.

In June 1948, when we stretched the tent for the first time, it measured 90 x 220 feet as compared to the present one which is 210 x 350 feet and seats 10,000. However, it looked huge to me and I wondered if we would ever see it filled to its capacity of 3,000.

The Durham Crusade opened with 700 present and closed three weeks later with a crowd exceeding 9,000 people. Thirty-seven people came to Christ the first night while more than 300 came the closing day.

A prominent Baptist layman from Durham was deeply moved by the healings he saw and he did much to break down prejudice against the crusade by certain denominational leaders. He answered the questions of an up-and-coming young Methodist pastor who had just graduated from Duke University Divinity School, and was destined to play a unique role in the charismatic revival now going on in historic churches and in our own ministry. His name was Tommy Tyson, and he is now serving as university minister at Oral Roberts University.

WE INCORPORATE OUR MINISTRY

By July of 1948 we incorporated the ministry. Evelyn and I had put several hundred dollars in a savings account—the first we had ever had. We drew it out and gave it to the attorneys and it became the nucleus for the ministry to be established financially.

In those days we were required to pay an advertising agency a full month in advance for our radio time. Since our expense offerings each week had not been sufficient, the only way the new corporation could guarantee the radio stations being paid was to give of our love offerings.

The Lord blessed us for doing this. It became a real joy to Evelyn and me as we saw our faith at work. Whatever we gave would come back to us, often multiplied beyond our dreams.

Office space in the little house on Main Street was soon bursting at the seams. I had foreseen this need and, by faith, had claimed an unimproved lot on South Boulder just a year before. With financial aid from a close friend, I was able to purchase the lot and build our first real office building.

I began my radio ministry in May 1947 on two radio stations.

14

The closing night crowd of the Miami, Florida Crusade in 1949. Rev. F. F. Bosworth and I are standing on the left. More than 1,300 people accepted Christ in this crusade, and scores were miraculously healed.

THE GREAT FLORIDA CRUSADES

The big tent was erected in Miami in January 1948 for the first of four crusades in the State of Florida. By the end of the first week, people had to come two hours early to get a seat! Thousands were saved and hundreds were miraculously healed.

A businessman from Whiteville, North Carolina flew his plane to Miami on a Friday night to be in the service. I did not know he was present, nor that he would later become my right arm in the business affairs of our ministry.

Here are a few things that happened that evening: the first young man prayed for had stammered all his life and it had hindered his career. After praying for him I turned him toward the audience and said, "The hardest place for a stammerer to talk is in front of an audience. If this young man is healed, he can talk before all of you and he will be able to express himself without stammering."

The boy's face was radiant with joy. Opening his mouth, he found that the words flowed. He was amazed. He would talk a while, then rejoice; talk some more and rejoice.

I knew exactly how he felt. I remembered the feeling of confidence that swept over me that glorious hour in 1935 when after the same kind of healing prayer, my stammering tongue was loosed.

An alcoholic man was healed next. As he felt the healing power of Christ, he cried, "Oral Roberts, what did you do to me?"

"I only prayed," I replied.

"Something is happening to me. It's like I am being made new."

"You have met Christ tonight," I said. "His presence is in you, healing and cleansing you from sin and from the desire for alcohol."

A naval officer returned to testify that evening. Only a few nights before he had been brought to the crusade dying with cancer. Facing me, he said, "Sir, I am healed of cancer. I have been under the care of Navy doctors for weeks. After prayer, I returned to the hospital, was X-rayed and pronounced completely free of cancer. It is a miracle! I also want to witness to an even greater miracle. I have been a very sinful man. Through this experience I have been converted to Christ and saved from my sins."

The following day Dr. Sproull, our crusade manager, introduced me to Lee Braxton, the businessman who had flown to Miami. I learned that he was mayor of his city, founder and president of the First National Bank there, and that he owned or held stock in several other businesses and corporations.

We shook hands and looked at each other. I was tall—he was short. I was 31 years old—he was 44. I was in the second year of the healing ministry, which was beginning now to move across America in a broad sweep—he was retiring. Lee told me of his impressions of the services: "I came to see if what I have been hearing is true," he said. "I decided if I liked what I saw, I would stay. If not, I would leave and no one would know the difference." He mentioned the healing of the stuttering boy, the alcoholic, and especially the naval officer's testimony. "But the thing that stirred my soul the most," he said, "was your preaching and the large number which came forward to be saved." He then asked, "What can I do to help you win souls?"

In the Early Church the Apostles selected outstanding laymen whom they appointed over the business of the ministry. I had already seen there was a business side of our ministry that had to be understood and handled. But how? No previous training had equipped me for the many complex things that had to be decided in handling thousands of people, in answering the mail that was already pouring in from throughout the nation, in securing radio time, in initiating and publishing a monthly magazine, in hiring personnel, in filling out reports and returns for the government, in making arrangements for travel, etc.

For the next several hours I asked him so many questions that he said later, "I had dealt with business and government leaders for the past 15 years, but I had never been asked as many questions by all of them as Oral Roberts asked me in one day."

Lee attended the Tampa, Jacksonville and Tallahassee Crusades that immediately followed Miami. He then flew to Tulsa with me and helped us organize our office on a businesslike basis. He also approached me on a plan to increase the number of radio stations carrying our broadcast to 100 stations. This was a goal I had been praying and working toward. It had seemed utterly impossible until this businessman came along and had the audacity to say it could be done.

I was glad to have Lee with me in the Tampa Crusade because I had to make a serious decision regarding the tent. By allowing people to stand around the edge of the tent seating 3,000, we could accommodate approximately 4,500. We needed a tent *seating* 4,500. This meant purchasing two more trailer trucks, 1,500 additional folding chairs, a larger portable platform and a new lighting system. Talk about needing good business judgment, I really needed it.

The Jacksonville Crusade was endorsed by the Mayor of the city. The Honorable C. Frank Whitehead testified that in answer to our prayer, he had been delivered from the cigarette habit. He also gave me a key to the city and asked that the Oral Roberts

Ft. Worth, Texas Crusade, June 1949. In this crusade 5,000 people responded to the invitation to receive Christ as their Savior, and more than 400 received the baptism with the Holy Spirit. Although the canvas cathedral could accommodate only 4,500, many of the people brought their own chairs. Others stood around the edge of the tent. On the final night of the crusade, approximately 11,000 people were present.

Crusade return to Jacksonville as soon as possible.

The really outstanding thing, however, was that all records were broken in winning converts. A total of 4,681 came to Christ!

I remember crowds standing up to 10 deep around the tent. Some of the healings are still vivid in my memory. A 17-year-old boy came to the service so violently tormented by demon power that it was necessary to strap him to a pole in the tent. After his deliverance he put his arms around me and said to his father, "I love Jesus now." I remember the little boy born without a hip socket, whom God touched, and the child was made whole. How this thrilled the audience! I remember the night when there was a spontaneous mass outpouring of healing power with people rushing forward from the audience to receive only a touch and to go away crying for joy that they had been healed. I remember one woman in particular in a wheelchair. I took her hand and said, "In the name of Jesus Christ of Nazareth, rise up and walk!" She rose, and pushed her own wheelchair from the tent.

We ended our Florida Crusade schedule in Tallahassee, Florida's capital city. "The beautiful old 'Majestic Lady', will never be the same again," reported the Reverend Carl C. Haas, crusade chairman. "We saw 7,873 souls come forward to accept Christ as their personal Savior, 1,100 of them in one single service! Never have we seen anything like this."

When we dismantled the tent and sent it on ahead to Norfolk, Virginia, there was little doubt that God had visited Florida and that multitudes would carry the word back to their homes across America that God still heals today, and there is a better life that can be had through faith in God.

"Escape of 7,000 called a miracle," reported Wes Ezzard of the Amarillo Times. In his editorial he spoke of the fatal night in Hartford, Connecticut, when fire swept through a circus tent where 7,000 were in attendance. Panic struck and 412 persons were injured and 107 died. Of the Amarillo disaster, he said: "There was no panic... confusion, yes... fear, but that deadly animal panic that strips men of reason was not present. Panic could have killed hundreds... the important thing is that most of the people in that tent were thinking about God, each in his own way, when disaster struck. And there was enough trust in God manifest there to prevent a deadly panic...."

THE FIFTIES
Living in a Miracle

One of my associates recently said, "Oral Roberts lives in a miracle on the edge of expectancy." Without miracles we could not have made it through the fifties.

In September 1950 we took the big tent to Amarillo, Texas. The Amarillo Crusade was glorious. More than 2,450 souls were saved. The miracles of healing were outstanding and thousands of people were moved with the presence and power of the Lord.

On the tenth night, a storm struck. The winds came roaring in out of the northwest. I was standing at the pulpit when suddenly the lights went out. I shouted, "Everyone stay seated and keep your mind on God!" They did. In the flashes of lightning, I saw the entire tent begin to lift toward the sky — it looked like billows of light — then begin to settle, floating down slowly.

"Oh, Lord, save the 7,000 people from harm!" I prayed.

It seemed as if a thousand invisible hands took control of the situation. The aluminum quarter poles fell very gently and the steel center poles, weighing 1,000 pounds each, seemed to be lowered a foot at a time. People began crawling out from under the tattered tent, fighting canvas off their heads.

I ran from group to group praying with people and praising God for their safety. It was several minutes before I realized that I did not know where Evelyn and little Richard Lee were. Later I learned they had taken shelter under the platform. When I found them, they were soaking wet, but safe. I took them to the car and went back to help the people.

When I saw I could do nothing more to help, I took Evelyn and the baby to our hotel room. After we dried ourselves, we sat by the radio listening to reports. The police and firemen were taking people to the hospitals. I said to Evelyn, "I don't think I can ever have a tent again where something like this might happen." When we received the last reports about four o'clock in the morning and knew that no one had been killed, we went to bed. The next morning the Amarillo *Times* ran a blazing headline: ESCAPE OF 7,000 CALLED MIRACLE. I immediately went to the hospital to see what could be done and to pray for the injured. I was encouraged when I learned that all but two people had been released. I prayed with them and God answered prayer. They later testified at another crusade that they had been healed.

IS THIS THE END?

I left the hospital and went to see the wreckage. There in the mud, I found my Bible, water-soaked and ruined. I stood amid the debris broken-hearted. Looking at the tattered remains of the tent, I wondered: *Am I finished? Is this the end?* Finally, I turned and walked slowly back to the car, where Evelyn was waiting. She handed me a stack of telegrams that had arrived that morning. They were from people who were praying for me, encouraging me to rise up and keep going on. Some said they would wire money for a new, bigger and better tent. For the first time tears came into my eyes. I looked at the tent and said, "Old Tent, you are gone, but I have no regrets. You fought the battle with me. Under your shelter more than 40,000 souls have come to Jesus."

"Lord," I said, "I have no regrets. I had nothing but faith when I started forty months ago. I still have that faith."

I had one more telegram to open. It was from a man in Colorado Springs, Colorado. It read, "Dear Brother Roberts, you can't go under for going over." Something leaped in my heart. I turned to Evelyn and said, "Honey, I am going to order a brand-new tent — a bigger and stronger tent, a tent that will stand the storms. Come on, let's go."

WE GO ON TELEVISION

In the early fifties, television was a struggling infant. You would see people clustered around a store window fascinated by this one-eyed genius. Few realized the impact it would make upon humanity.

At that time there were 26 million television sets in the United States and the number was growing every day. God showed me the potential of using television for our ministry. Now, for the first time in history, the Gospel of deliverance could be preached directly to sinners in their homes and in many public places where unsaved people congregate.

There were predictions that radio would overshadow television. We did not believe this. We were on 300 powerful radio stations in the United States and overseas and were receiving a very good response. However, we felt God was also directing us to use television. It was *new* and *exciting;* people were captivated by it and anxious to watch. We recognized that many would watch a program who would not just listen.

We also considered television as a means of follow-up. Many people became convicted of their sins during the crusades but did not fully surrender their lives to God. We believed it would cause these people to go on with God and accept Him fully. Others who were not completely healed could receive further help through watching the program.

For at least three years, we continued to pray and seek God's will. I was determined that when I made the move it would be divinely ordained of God.

Finally, we believed, the time had come. After weeks of hard work, our first television program was premiered on January 10, 1954, on 16 stations. Others were quickly added as time could be cleared and pledges of support were received.

The response was immediate. Overnight, our volume of mail soared. This confirmed our convictions that we were heading in the right direction.

Yet, there was something lacking. The programs, being filmed in a studio, had no live crusade audience to "pull" the message out of me. I felt the people were not getting the real power and impact of the deliverance ministry. We investigated the possibilities of televising our crusades live. A major television network visited a crusade and told us it could not be done. Rex Humbard of Akron, Ohio encouraged us to find a way to film directly from the tent. Finally, we located a film company who agreed to try it for $42,000. Besides conquering the mechanical and technical difficulties involved with filming, we had to do a selling job with our audiences. Some felt it was sacrilegious to bring the cameras into the sacred confines of the service. I told them that if they would cooperate by worshipping God and ignoring the cameras, we would have a chance to capture on film the true spirit of the crusade.

"If God's anointing is on us here," I said, "it will be on the film. When people view it, it will have the same effect on them as it does on you." The filming went well. The people were with me 100 percent. The Lord anointed me in a powerful way.

Fred O'Dell's healing was one of the first miracles to be recorded on film for television. He says, "On April 5, 1955, I was healed of incurable cancer of the lymph glands. I had become ill in January of that year. In February, the doctors told me they could do nothing for me and gave me six months to live. My wife insisted that I go to the Jacksonville Crusade. At the time, I was not a believer, but I went to the crusade and remained for five days.

"When my time for prayer came, you interviewed me; then you laid your hands on me and prayed. The first time you prayed, apparently nothing happened—then you prayed again. I was completely consumed in the Spirit and I swung around and faced the audience, you were holding my hand at the time. Then I saw the hand of Jesus, from the elbows down, placed over my hand and His fingers placed downward over my body. I saw the nail prints there and the blood running from His hand. My wife, who was in the audience, said my face was as red as blood. The only explanation I have is that this was the blood of Jesus healing me of that awful cancer. I am still healed today from the soles of my feet to the crown of my head."

In 1952, we filmed "Venture Into Faith," capturing for tens of thousands the spiritual blessing of a crusade. As our associates traveled across the United States and overseas to Africa and the Philippines showing this film, thousands of men and women were saved and healed. In just a month's showing behind the Iron Curtain, 6,000 people accepted Christ. Altogether more than 250,000 people have come to know Christ as their Savior through this evangelistic outreach.

GOD GIVES ME A PLAN

God gave me a plan — the Blessing Pact — to finance the television film.

I called a special afternoon service and shared this plan with my partners. I told them the Lord had given me a plan to enter into a partnership with each person who would help me to carry on our ministry. This partnership would be called a *Blessing Pact*. I pointed out examples of this in the Bible. The widow of Zarapheth entered into a blessing pact with the Prophet Elijah when she grasped the principle of partnership with God — that it is based upon faith and miracles. She had to do something first, even though it was just a little. Then God performed a miracle for her in return and supplied her needs in abundance. The disciples entered into a blessing pact with Jesus when they let Him borrow their boat to preach the Gospel. When the discouraged disciples launched out at the Lord's command and cast their nets, they became partners with God and He blessed them with a boat-sinking, net-breaking load.

Then I dropped a bombshell into their thinking. I said, "If I can trust God for the $42,000 to film the crusade, can you trust Him for $100? I am asking 420 people in this audience to make this pledge and, in turn, let me, as an instrument of God, enter into a Blessing Pact with you for one year. I will use your gift to win souls; and because of this, I will earnestly pray that the Lord will return your gift in its entirety from a totally unexpected source." I promised if at the end of one year, God had not blessed them, I would return their money.

There was an audible gasp in the audience. The audacity of such a plan shook me a little, too. But I knew God had given me the plan and I felt it would open the doors of their minds to thinking and believing for bigger things in their own lives.

Approximately 420 stood to accept the challenge and became the first members of the Blessing Pact.

Once again God vindicated this step of faith. My partners testified by the hundreds how God blessed and prospered them through the Blessing Pact. Shortly there-after we were able to withdraw our guarantee, for God was doing more than we had ever expected.

I could tell you about Blessing Pact Partners who are fruit growers up in Oregon, whose outstanding crops have been the talk of the entire area since they joined the Blessing Pact; the man from Indiana, who was a local insurance representative when he joined the Blessing Pact, and in a matter of months was promoted to general agent of northeastern Indiana; or the California botanist who received a call one hour after he mailed his first check to the Blessing Pact. The county was interested in an old gravel pit he had on his property. They paid him over a thousand dollars for the gravel. I could introduce you to many who have attributed their healing, the salvation of loved ones and the restoration of broken homes to the Blessing Pact as the instrument they used to release their faith.

10 MILLION FRONT-ROW SEATS

In February 1955, we televised our first *live* service. Little did we realize that eleven years later we would be on more than 100 television stations, blanketing North America with this message of salvation and deliverance.

A young man from the West Coast, Mr. Fred O'Dell, was one of the first to be prayed for in the filmings. Dying with cancer, he flew all the way to Jacksonville, Florida, to enter the prayer line not knowing it would be filmed. I said to him, "All we want you to do when you receive prayer is to be natural. Pay no attention to the cameras. Should you be healed, the cameras will record it and millions will see it and be inspired to believe for their healing."

We discovered that Fred was so desperate and so intent on believing God for his healing that he was unaware of anything but the laying on of hands. That was his point of contact for the releasing of his faith. There is no way to estimate the vast number of people who were tuned in when Fred's healing was shown on TV. A year later we brought him back. His second appearance on TV, along with X-ray proof, showed him to

The healing of Anna Williams was a miracle that quickened the pulse of the nation. On Sunday afternoon, May 1, 1955, at 1:53 p.m., 22-year-old Anna Williams, the invalid wife of Bill Williams, an Air Force sergeant, was healed while watching our television program. The news of this miracle swept the country from coast to coast. The Wichita Falls Beacon carried the story. With headlines and pictures, it proclaimed, ANNA WILLIAMS HEALED. From here, the story winged its way across the nation in nearly every major newspaper — Los Angeles, Chicago, Oklahoma City, Dallas, and New York. In the picture, Bill looks adoringly at his wife who had been a cripple all their married lives — but is now healed by God's power.

be restored in weight and strength, a well man.

Some of the most marvelous healings in this ministry have never been shown because a piece of TV equipment failed and the last minute or two of the healing was not captured on film. When this has happened, I have actually broken down and wept.

Our telecasts have given a front-row seat in the crusades to millions who might never have attended otherwise.

When the team and I were received by the late John F. Kennedy in the White House, he said, "Reverend Roberts, I've seen you on television and I enjoy it very much."

A United States senator told me he had renewed his faith in God while watching one of the telecasts.

The Reverend Warren Hultgren, pastor of the First Baptist Church in Tulsa, and a warm friend, introduced me to speak to Tulsa Rotary Club of which I am a member. He said, "I was in New York recently and rode in from the airport in a cab. The driver was very talkative. He finally asked me where I was from. When I said, 'Tulsa', he almost lost control of the cab.

"'Let me ask you something', he said. 'Every week my old lady writes Oral Roberts for prayer. Sometimes she sends a little money along. Tell me, is that guy on the level?'

"'I believe Oral Roberts to be a sincere man of God who is doing great good in the world', I answered.

"He said, 'Am I relieved to hear that. You know, I've been secretly watching him on TV myself."

Wherever I go I meet people who tell me they accepted Christ while watching the program. Others relate how they were healed. Ministers have shared how seeing an actual healing caused them to re-study Jesus to reexamine their own ministry. Only eternity will reveal the total results of our television ministry.

MASTER PLAN
FOR 10 MILLION SOULS

In December 1953, God spoke to me and said: *You are to win a million souls in the next 36 months.* I staggered and reeled under this command. For a moment I didn't

"Enlarge the place of thy tent" (Isaiah 54:2). The medium of television has become a tent-enlarger to our crusades. It has opened a whole new era of deliverance to millions across the world who live in need of abundant life.

In 1959, during our third trip to Israel, I was received by Prime Minister Ben Gurion. He impressed me as a man attempting to lead his people with all the wisdom and understanding he possessed.

We quickly outgrew our first office building. Construction on the second building began in April 1953, and we moved in August 1954.

know what to do. Never before had anyone been asked to win a million souls in 36 short months! How could I do it? I could not do it alone.

So I called our first World Outreach Conference. Only a small handful of my partners were in that first conference, but when I presented the challenge to them, they were moved with the same spirit I felt. I owe my partners so much! With their faithful support we were able to win the first million souls — not in the 3 years allotted, but in 29½ months!

We rejoiced in this, but we were to receive an even greater challenge.

We were in Hong Kong in January 1956. There we met with several missionaries for prayer. While we were praying I heard the voice of the Lord calling my name. Very quietly the Lord said, *Son, if you will seek My pleasure, My joy and My faith, I will give you ten million souls in ten years.* It was a number much greater than I had ever dreamed possible.

I returned to my room, opened my Bible, and began to study and pray. I called my team together and shared the experience with them. We fell on our knees and began to seek God for further guidance.

The Lord showed us that first, I was to seek God's pleasure. He gave me the Scripture, "The Lord takes no pleasure in the death of the wicked." The saving of souls is God's pleasure.

Second, I was to seek the joy of the Lord. He gave me the Scripture, "The joy of the Lord is your strength." He said, "That is why you have grown weak in body while overseas. That is why you are burdened." I knew I had lost part of my joy in the Manila Crusade because I could not get across to the people what I was trying to say until the last part of the meeting.

The Lord was saying, "The joy of the Lord is your strength. You seek My joy and you will be strong the rest of your life."

Third, He said, "Seek my faith." I thought, *What is the faith of God?* Then He showed me what He meant. He said, "Oral Roberts, you are trying to be an American preacher. You think that no one can be saved in large numbers except the American people. My Son died for all." God certainly enlarged my vision that day.

He gave me a Master Plan to win 10 million souls to Jesus Christ — our Seven World Outreaches. These outreaches include: (1) crusades, (2) overseas ministry, (3) radio and television, (4) Hebrew Bibles, (5) North American Indians, (6) Abundant Life Prayer Group and (7) literature.

The Master Plan gave us the means to proclaim the Gospel to our generation within our lifetime.

Our Second Million Souls Crusade began in January 1956 and was completed in 14½ months. In March 1957 the Third Crusade was launched, and 12 months later another million souls won to Christ was announced by our Auditing Department. When we announced in 1958 our desire to win the Fourth Million Souls to Jesus Christ in twelve months, we faced a tremendous challenge. But, to God be the glory, the task was not beyond the reach of faith.

In the succeeding years, the ministry has continued to win millions to Christ through its worldwide outreaches.

There is an excitement in the tent crusades that we don't always experience in our auditorium meetings. The aura of hope and expectancy is contagious. Many miracles have been wrought, and millions of people have come to know Jesus of Nazareth as their personal Savior in the "tent cathedral."

I especially wanted to film for our television audiences the ruins of this synagogue in the ancient city of Capernaum. Jesus preached here and also delivered a man of an unclean spirit. (Mark 1:21-29.)

WALKING WHERE JESUS WALKED

One of my most thrilling experiences has been to visit the Holy Land—there to retrace the steps of Jesus of Nazareth. Because of the spiritual blessing to my life, I decided to film these sacred scenes for our television audience. In 1955 we filmed the Easter and Christmas stories. Then in 1959 we returned to film the land and people and to show the effect of our World Outreach program of Hebrew Bible distribution.

The one place I especially wanted to film was the ruins of the synagogue in the ancient city of Capernaum. Jesus had preached in the synagogue at Capernaum and also delivered a man of an unclean spirit. (Mark 1:21-28.) The ruins were now under the jurisdiction of one of the historic churches; however, I was given permission to preach to a group of Jewish people who came over from Tiberias for the filming. When I was about three-fourths finished, there was a loud cry, "Stop! Stop!" I looked around and saw a man running toward me where I stood on a big stone near the synagogue wall.

Above the murmur of the audience, I asked, "Why are you stopping us? We secured permission to film my message to these people here."

"I have authority over this place," he replied, "and you cannot film further."

There was a stir in the crowd and for a few moments it appeared there might be violence. I asked the crowd to be calm. Suddenly there was a commotion at our cameras. Several of the religious leaders were attacking the cameramen in an effort to destroy the film that had been taken. Only the intervention of their leader saved the scenes we had already made and kept them from breaking up the equipment.

My Jewish audience wanted me to continue preaching, and a leading man among them offered to phone the government in Jerusalem. I realized, however, we were on private property and although we had permission, I did not want to cause trouble. I asked the crowd to disperse and the cameramen to remove their equipment from the synagogue floor.

Fortunately, enough film had been taken to make sense from the sermon I was preaching and we were able to use it on television.

Wembley Stadium was the site of the crusade for the white people of Johannesburg, South Africa. Here I experienced the thrill of a lifetime. On Saturday night of this crusade, 5,000 people responded to the invitation to accept Christ. This was the largest altar response God had ever given me up to that time. It was a beautiful sight!

SOUTH AFRICA

As I have traveled throughout the world conducting crusades, one of the things that stands out in my mind is that people everywhere are the same. They have different backgrounds, cultures and habits, but inwardly people are the same. They have the same desire for God, the same urge to release their faith for miracles and the same ambition to rise above their limitations. The key to reaching these people is the love of God.

My first service in South Africa was worth all the hard, weary miles I traveled. Before the first mass meeting in Wembley Stadium, I was taken by car to preach to a very large crowd of natives who had heard of our ministry through the film, "Venture Into Faith."

When I entered the grove of trees where they were singing a hymn, their eyes shone with excitement. I had spoken only a few minutes when I discerned that they were ready to be saved and healed. Literally hundreds of hands went up, indicating a desire to be saved, after which they thronged me for prayer. One young woman was instantly healed of a broken neck. She pulled off her brace and gave it to me. The audience shouted and cried for joy, some clapping their hands. After this, they pressed so close that it seemed I would never be able to minister to them all.

An important outreach of our ministry is the giving of Hebrew Bibles (both Old and New Testaments to the Jewish people. When I was in Israel in 195; I talked with a group of Galilean fishermen and gav them personally autographed copies of th Hebrew Bible.

OUR LARGEST ALTAR CALL

Wembley Stadium was the site of the crusade for the white people of Johannesburg. A shelter was built over my head, but the stadium, except for 7,000 seats under cover, was open-air. The first night there was a downpour of rain. Nevertheless, thousands were present. I preached in my raincoat, and more than 500 people came forward in the rain to be saved. This was followed by the prayer line with many spectacular healings.

Saturday night I felt impressed to preach the sermon, "A Man's Life." I wondered, would it work in South Africa? Would the conservative Dutch and English respond to it? When I reached the part where God gave me the vision of the worth of one soul, no matter what the color of the skin was, would they, in the land where they are wrestling with a severe racial problem, not take offense?

For one hour and a half I preached on what a man is and what he is worth—then the altar call. Twenty-thousand people were seated in front and back of the pulpit. It was a beautiful sight. While every head was bowed, I quickly asked all who wanted to be genuinely saved and born again to raise their hands. Thousands of hands went up and I knew it was going to be the largest altar call God had ever given me. I asked them to stand and come forward quickly. Although there was a space roughly 50 by 400 feet in front of the platform, it wasn't nearly large enough. They streamed down the aisles and out of the grandstands. More than 5,000 came forward to make confession of Jesus Christ of Nazareth!

The chairman of the crusade said, "Brother Roberts, if your ministry does no more than this in Africa, it is well worth the entire crusade." I knew what he meant. I, too, was thrilled at what God was doing night after night, but I said, "My work is only begun. Come with me."

PRAYING WITH THE LEPERS

We went down under the bleachers where the invalids had been brought. After I had laid hands upon more than 100 desperate people, I was asked to come into a little anteroom where about 20 lepers were waiting.

Will I ever forget those lepers? I saw men and women with their bodies partially eaten away. Where a hand used to be, there was only a stub. Part of a face was gone. One man had lost a foot. It broke me up.

The thought came, *If you lay hands on these people, you might take leprosy. Then what will become of your ministry?*

I have always found it rather easy to stand before an audience and preach, although it takes much preparation, quite a bit of courage and the anointing of the Holy Spirit. I have found it much more difficult to leave the pulpit and go down where the sick and suffering are and risk my whole ministry in what might happen as I pray for them. It is pretty safe to preach but it is rather risky to invade the citadel of Satan's power where people are held in the bondage of demons, fear and disease.

Ruth Peffer, a school teacher in Johannesburg, South Africa, was instantly healed of a broken neck in our crusade there in 1955.

At first I felt like cringing. Then I felt like running away and saying, "What does all this have to do with me?" But I could not run. Healing is not something that I can take or leave. I cannot be neutral about it. It reached me in the extremity of my young life and through it Christ delivered me. Squaring my shoulders, I walked toward the lepers and began to lay hands upon them and pray in the name of Jesus Christ. Some stood solid and unmoving. It was difficult to tell if they were responding or not. Others received my prayers as if I were an angel sent from God, their faces lighting up in smiles and words of praise to God flowing from their lips.

This experience tendered my heart and did something to my inner man.

A committee was formed in South Africa to promote a crusade to win 100,000 souls in 1955. An office was established there to take care of the mail that came in to us. We sent the Committee all of our literature, including tracts and AMERICA'S HEALING MAGAZINE (now known as ABUNDANT LIFE), tape recordings, the "Venture Into Faith" film, television films, projectors and tape recorders. This was handled by representatives of the sponsoring churches under the direction of the South Africa Committee.

SOUTHERN RHODESIA

In 1959 we carried the message of Christ's deliverance into the virgin territory of Salisbury, Southern Rhodesia, South Africa, where we conducted an intensive three-day crusade. There the giant tobacco Auctions, Ltd., warehouse — one of the world's largest — was converted for use as a house of God.

Our crusade was the first revival program of such magnitude to come to this section of Rhodesia, and there were many who doubted that large crowds would attend the tobacco floors for the meeting. These doubts were short-lived. The first afternoon service saw some 4,000 people present and a spirit of expectancy and enthusiasm rising from the throng to greet Bob DeWeese as he stepped forward to conduct the meeting. The Salisbury Crusade was marked by this marvelous spirit of faith and expectancy throughout.

It was a real thrill to personally distribute our literature to the "red-blanket people" of the Transkei area. Actually the blankets are orange-colored and denote tribal connections. Hundreds of these Africans responded to the invitation to accept Christ.

THE RED-BLANKET PEOPLE

During this same trip we visited the Transkei area. The *Transkei* is a section of country south of Durban. The name comes from the word *Kei*, which is the name of a river, and, of course, Transkei is across the Kei. This section of country is inhabited by one and one-half million natives. At least fifty percent of the natives wore the characteristic orange-colored blanket which they dye themselves. They are called the "red-blanket people," and they are very picturesque. The red blanket denotes the native's tribal connection.

It was estimated that there were about 11,000 natives at this final meeting. We were told by the workers that never had such a meeting been held in Transkei. The fact that hundreds and thousands of these red-blanket people were willing to raise their hands for prayer and stand up in public and accept Christ in sight of their neighbors and friends, was a very great forward step.

A national pastor said to me, "Brother Roberts, these natives are accustomed to the black man's power of witchcraft and the power of their witch doctors — power that seems at times to be supernatural. They have never seen the power of the white man's God. You are the first man in the Transkei who has ever performed things like this by the power of God, and these people are really amazed."

The city fathers of both Sydney and Melbourne granted us free use of their beautiful parks for our tent crusade. Thousands crowded the big tent night after night to hear the Gospel of deliverance, and to see the miracles of God.

PERSECUTION IN AUSTRALIA

The miraculous power of God is a direct frontal attack on the kingdom of Satan to loose the captive, to bring deliverance to the oppressed. In Australia we saw Satan's counterattack.

We went there on the invitation of a group of ministers representing the Full Gospel Churches and by the authority of the Australian Government.

The city fathers of both Sydney and Melbourne granted us free use of their beautiful city parks for the big eight-pole tent. The people were hungry for God. It was a most natural setting for a great crusade.

But, acting under some strange influence, some of the daily newspapers of the two cities had decided that we would not have successful meetings in Australia. Obviously prewritten stories greeted us as the first crusade opened in Sydney. Later, a few half-truths, were sprinkled in to give the stories the appearance of factual reporting. A reporter, who was reproved by a minister for this travesty of reporting said, "We are not writing what we want to write, but what we are told to write."

The main body of people who came were eager, open and ready for the Gospel. They represented many of the Australian churches.

During the ten days, approximately 75,000 attended. The power of God was seen as hundreds decided to follow Christ. Many testified to miraculous healings.

The police cooperated splendidly and instructed our workers in the handling of the large crowds. Order was maintained and, with little exception, the people were reverent and impressed. Approximately 3,000 people came forward in 10 nights to give their hearts to God. Of the altar calls, our Australian representative said, "We have just seen the largest altar calls in Australia's history."

The Melbourne meeting started off on an even larger scale than Sydney. It looked as though it might be the greatest opening night of all our crusades. Four hundred came forward for salvation. A nurse who had come hundreds of miles for prayer for deformed feet was marvelously healed.

The next morning (Monday), the Melbourne newspapers launched an all-out attack. Every conceivable ruse was used to mislead the people and keep them away from the meeting.

On Monday night, heckling started during the service. People yelled out to interrupt during the preaching and prayer for the sick.

By Wednesday night, it was obvious that the opposition was organized. Hecklers, who came to the front with the converts, yelled and screamed their defiance. Well-known Communist agitators were recognized moving about, stirring up the mob.

From the very start of the crusade the response to the altar calls had been tremendous. But, by Wednesday, with the mob defying anyone to accept Christ as their personal Savior, only about sixty brave souls came forward. It was then that I realized the mob was not against me, for when they hissed the Word of God and defied sinners to receive Christ as their personal Savior, I saw that they were anti-God and anti-religion.

After the service was dismissed, the mob rushed to the back of the tent to get me, but I had already been rushed off the grounds with a police escort. That night one of our trucks was set on fire and one rope on the big tent was cut. (It was uncanny that a news photographer "just happened" to be present to photograph the vandalism.) That night they "booed" and tried to turn over the car that Evelyn was sitting in because they thought I was in it. When they found I wasn't, they quit. Later, Evelyn said to me, "Oral, I don't want you to stay. They are going to do something terrible and someone is going to get hurt. I wish you would close the meeting and leave." I replied, "Honey, as long as the people are getting saved and healed, I can't leave."

Threats of physical violence had been made on my life. Several times Evelyn received phone calls saying, "If you want your husband alive, get him out of Australia because we are going to see that he doesn't live if he stays here."

The next day before I awakened, the team read the early morning headlines: "FIRE SET AT ORAL ROBERTS' TENT . . . TO-

Healed in the Sydney Crusade was 11-year-old Helen Barrett, a victim of polio. At the 1966 World Congress on Evangelism in Berlin, a Presbyterian minister from Australia said, "I have recently seen Helen. She is still healed; she is now married and is a fine Christian mother."

Press photographers crouched on the platform within a few feet of me while I was preaching. They refused to move.

NIGHT IT IS GOING TO BE BURNED DOWN." It was then that they made the decision to close the crusade based on the Scripture in Acts 19:30-31: *And when Paul would have entered in unto the people, the disciples suffered him not. And certain of the chief of Asia, which were his friends, sent unto him, desiring him that he would not adventure himself into the theatre.*

The team did not feel that it was wise to endanger my life further. Also, they felt that we could not continue the crusade through Sunday and jeopardize the lives of thousands of innocent people.

When the team told me of their decision, they handed me plane tickets to America and advised me that the tent had already been dismantled and was on its way to the ship.

The Melbourne Crusade was over but in many ways it had a victorious ending. It caught an antagonistic press by surprise. The full responsibility was thrown into the lap of the newspapers who stirred up and supported the mobs. They could not deny their guilt, for all Australia had been watching their reports.

The greatest good was the fact that it brought to light the power of a Communist minority in Australia. It underlined the fact that true religious liberty was not known there. It set in motion a drive to get a law passed to guarantee individual freedom to worship God according to the dictates of one's conscience.

OUR MINISTRY CONTINUES IN AUSTRALIA

Today, eight Australian stations carry our radio broadcast. We maintain overseas offices in Australia as well as in New Zealand, South Africa, South India, British Isles and Canada. Recently Norman Armstrong, manager of the Australian work, sent our office this encouraging report: "Whether in the great cities or on the isolated aboriginal reserves, we are constantly finding lives that have been transformed and are meeting people who have been miraculously healed through this ministry.

"The work in this country is backed by a faithful team of 600 Blessing-Pact Partners and a special prayer band who combine to make this ministry here a mighty force for God.

"Thousands of miles are traveled each year as we take this ministry personally to unreached areas, screening the films and ministering to the people. Millions of pieces of Abundant Life literature have been distributed throughout this land, bearing the good tidings of God's delivering power.

"Australia has not yet felt the full impact of the charismatic renewal being so wonderfully experienced in other countries, but Brother Roberts' ministry is helping to prepare the groundwork. His clear, anointed messages on radio, making so vivid the place and work of the Holy Spirit in the life of Christians and the Church today, is touching people from all religious backgrounds. God is using this ministry in a mighty way to bless this great land 'down under.'"

In Manila, we were introduced to President Ramon Magsaysay. As we talked, he impressed me as a deeply spiritual man. I had the privilege of praying with him before I left.

Our crusade equipment being hoisted aboard an ocean-going liner enroute to Australia.

The people of the Philippines thronged our Manila Crusade. This is about one-third of one audience. Thousands sat on the ground each night to hear the Gospel because there were no chairs. In only eight services, approximately 25,000 came for salvation.

At the groundbreaking for the Abundant Life Building, Oklahoma's former Governor Gary said: "This great Oral Roberts organization is a miracle within itself. It would be impossible for a man by himself to go out and within a period of ten years, or even an entire lifetime, set up such an organization. For he carries the message of the Lord to more than half of the countries of the world . . . you can't do that by yourself . . . you have to have help from our Father in Heaven. Oral Roberts has had that — and has it now."

I FACE ABSOLUTE DEFEAT

I vividly remember a period during late 1957 and early 1958 when a shortage of funds threatened to stop our ministry entirely.

The Abundant Life Office was being constructed in Tulsa. This beautiful seven-story building was going up when suddenly our loan did not come through. A recession had struck our nation and we suffered in that same recession. Lending institutions of the country withdrew many of their commitments, and we were included in the "cutback."

One million dollars had been promised us by the bank. Lee Braxton and I went up to sign for it and were told that they had made no commitment to us at all!

Lee looked at me and I looked at him. Were we dreaming when we had sat in this same office months before and were told we had a commitment for one million dollars? There was no need to argue, the conversation was over, and we left.

For the next three months I faced absolute defeat. Since we began we have never defaulted an obligation. This is part of the integrity on which this ministry has been built. The outer walls of the building were up and that was all. We had been paying as we built. Now there were no funds left and seemingly we could borrow none.

Lee Braxton and his wife, Norma, offered their entire estate with no strings attached. Their offer brought tears to my eyes but I turned them down. I am so glad I did. However, the wonderful spirit of their offer lifted my faith.

One day Manford Engel, our vice-president, phoned me during a crusade. "Oral, I dislike to disturb you during a crusade," he said, "but we are out of funds. May we have your permission to shut down construction of the new building?"

"Manford," I replied, "I have no instructions from the Lord to halt construction. He has told me to build and I must obey."

"Then a miracle must take place immediately," he answered.

The crusade ended and I returned home.

I went at once to the site of the Abundant Life Building. It was winter and the weather was bad. I stood across the street and looked at what God told me to build. To the physical eyes it was only a skeleton of a building.

The Devil whispered, "You are looking at 'Oral Roberts' folly'. This is all the people will ever see as they pass by."

The icy winds whipped around me and I shivered in the cold. But I shut my eyes and ears to the Devil's suggestions, pulled my coat collar up around my head and began to pray.

Suddenly a glowing radiance surrounded my being, for as I prayed I felt the presence of Jesus of Nazareth. All at once it was like a vision before me! The building was finished in gleaming white, the different departments were staffed and workers were sending literature, radio tapes, TV films and letters throughout the world. In a flash I was in Japan, India and other faraway countries. People were saying, "Oral Roberts, when are you coming to us with your messages and prayers?" I saw myself in these nations reaping a harvest of souls for the Master.

Before the vision vanished, God reaffirmed to me that I had been born for this purpose and was raised up for this hour to take the message of His healing power to my generation.

When I opened my eyes the weather was

At one period, during late 1957, a shortage of funds created a real crisis while we were in the process of building the Abundant Life Building. I stood across the street and looked at the partially finished structure, and the devil whispered, "You are looking at 'Oral Roberts' folly'." Then God gave me a vision of the nations of the world in need of this abundant life message. When the vision was finished, I opened my eyes. Nothing had changed, but my heart was changed. I knew we were in the stream of God's purpose and that God would give us a miracle—and that miracle came!

Standing in front of the completed Abundant Life Building, I asked God to bless and hallow this place. We dedicated it to the glory of God and for the winning of souls to Jesus Christ. At the conclusion of my prayer, former Governor J. Howard Edmondson (left) cut the ribbon across the door, officially opening the new International Headquarters of our ministry. Evelyn stands behind me, and Tulsa's former Mayor James Maxwell is to her right.

still cold and dreary, the building was only a shell and I was alone on the side of the street. Yet I was not alone, for Jesus was with me. A miracle had begun to happen in my heart.

I knew that cold day a miracle would happen. There was no longer the nagging torment of doubt and anxiety. *I knew*. The gift of faith was at work. And, that miracle came!

I was in the next crusade when Mr. Engel telephoned: "I am calling to give you the good news!" he said. "Two things are happening: first, special contributions for the Abundant Life Building are coming in from friends and partners everywhere; second, the largest lending institution in Tulsa has extended us a line of credit, which, with the contributions coming in, will enable us to finish construction on schedule." His voice was hoarse with emotion as he continued, "I am so full I can hardly talk. I knew you would want to be the first to know."

"Yes," I replied, "I already knew it."

"Why, this just happened," he exclaimed, "how *could* you know?"

"I don't mean I knew of this transaction," I said. "I mean I knew God would supply the need. I have known since I stood across the street and prayed."

Manford began praising God over the phone and I joined him.

In May 1959, the Abundant Life Building was dedicated as our international headquarters for soul-winning.

While participating in the dedication ceremonies, Oklahoma's Governor, the Honorable J. Howard Edmondson, said, "I think today we have here something much more than the dedication of a most magnificent building. It is also a symbol of something of which Tulsans, Oklahomans and anyone else, can be proud. There is a tremendous void in the world today with reference to genuine faith.

This building is a monument to the efforts of a man who is contributing much to the filling of that void with faith in the hearts and minds of men throughout the earth."

Gratefully, we dedicated the Abundant Life Building to prayer and faith, to be an instrument in the hands of God to carry the message of deliverance to the world.

Of the Abundant Life Building, Oklahoma's former Governor J. Howard Edmondson said, "I think today we have here something much more than the dedication of a most magnificent building. It is also a symbol of something of which Tulsans, Oklahomans and everyone else can be proud. This building is a monument to the efforts of a man who is contributing much to fill a void of faith in the hearts and minds of men throughout the earth."

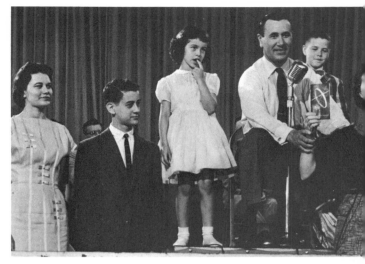

Rarely have I had opportunity to have the entire family with me in the crusades. This was taken in 1957 during the Trenton Crusade.

Our sons, Ronald David and Richard Lee, in the early 50's displaying real "brotherly love."

Daily Blessing, our devotional magazine, was first published in March 1959. Today, over a quarter of a million people are drawing spiritual strength from this highly inspirational publication.

One of the highlights of our ministry was the 1957 Los Angeles Crusade. The final service was held in the world-famous Hollywood Bowl. More than 3,000 people responded to the invitation to accept Christ as Savior the night this photograph was taken!

General Mark Clark invited the team and me to visit The Citadel (the military college of S. C.) during our crusade in Charleston, South Carolina. I still treasure the memories of my visit and the cordial reception at The Citadel. We enjoyed "southern hospitality" at its finest.

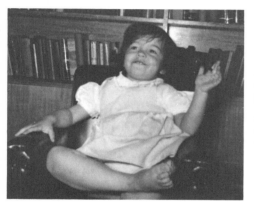

This 1954 picture candidly portrays Roberta, our youngest, a real little charmer, isn't she?

Honorable Kerr Scott, Governor of North Carolina, talks with me after giving a brief address to the audience of Fayetteville, N. C. Crusade. "The power of the Man of Galilee is available to us today," he said as he warmly welcomed our crusade.

"The Lord has been so very good to me to give me such a wonderful companion," says Evelyn. *"A little girl once asked me, 'How does it feel to live with a man of God?' I answered, 'I can't imagine living any other kind of life except one with this man of God—Oral Roberts.' Yet, these letters tell better than I can what kind of husband and father Oral is....'"*

EVELYN'S KEEPSAKES

(Written from summer camp)

Dear Mother

I want to please come home when this week is over. I am not homesick, but I don't like this place very much. Please come, and get me Sat. the 4. PLEASE! PLEASE! PLEASE! PLEASE!

I want to come home Sat.

Ronnie
Roberta

Sept. 16, 1955
Los Angeles, Calif.

My dearest darling Evelyn,

I've never has such a completely relaxing good time and rest AND besides the rest, I had you, the sweetest and best girl a man ever had.

This has been 2 weeks of soul searching, of reaching for the Lord, of realizing that my most pressing need is more of the Lord —especially in discerning, in the ability to see through people and things. I dreamed a dream last night that clears up one thing—the Lord showed me my battle is not with man but with demons, and that the battle is to be joined at once.

This has been a good day, tomorrow the crusade (Orange County) starts and I am fully ready.

Last night I had the team out to eat. They gave us a room and after eating we had a time of testifying and praying. I spoke on Jesus of Nazareth, and all of us felt He was there.

It seems there is a door about to be opened and I am eager to enter it.

I love you, Evelyn—and I love my children. You are very dear and precious to me. We have to be separated, but it is for the Gospel's sake. Because we love the Lord, we can stand it.

Tell Rebecca I love her. Tell Ronnie I love him. Kiss Richard and Roberta, and tell them I love them. Tell them I am praying for them—and you, too—always.

The Lord bless you, Evelyn, and keep you. With all my love, I am

Yours forever,
Oral

BAKERSFIELD INN
Bakersfield, California

Sat. noon

Dearest Evelyn—
So good to hear your very sweet voice last night. You are still my "sweetheart." Never have you been more my precious darling. The children mean increasingly more to me. I guess I'm just "high" on my family. I'm a one-woman, one-family man.

Things are looking up for a great meeting here. We've never had a finer opening service—they worship like real southerners.

Evelyn, suppose you and Lillie Mae plan to come out here next Saturday, staying thru the meeting....

Have Bill to let Mrs. Fahnestock do some of her work at our house while she keeps the children; he can pick it up every day or two. Also have him to hire some "extra" or special help to wrap the magazine.

Our payments at the bank are due the 7th of each month. Kiss the 3 R's for me.

Just your loving husband,
Oral

DORIC TACOMA Motor Hotel

Fourth and St. Helens
Tacoma 3, Washington
FUlton 3-2711

125 Deluxe Units; Heated Po[ol]
Shops, Restaurants, Lounge,
Banquet Facilities.
Ample Free Parking

Dear Richard:
I am writing you this letter to tell you that I love you. I am proud to have a son like you. It seems that you are growing dearer to me all the time.

It pleases and thrills me to see that you love Jesus . . . and that you love to go to church . . . and love to read your Bible. Just keep it up and God will always guide you.

Rich, really apply yourself in school. Do your very, very best. I am praying for you.

I love you,
Daddy

VIA AIR MAIL — CORREO AERE[O]

My dearest Evelyn and children:
At last! This is my dream.

I am on my way to walk the dusty roads of Israel and try to catch a little more of His Spirit and make it mine. Some new touch, some new understanding, some new contact—so I won't fail so much.

I intend to climb Calvary—slowly.

Stand on Olives' brow where His feet last touched earth. Go into the Upper Room where the "sound like a rushing mighty wind" came. Sit at the Beautiful gate where the lame man "leaped and walked" and on the Jericho Road where blind Bartimaeus received his sight.

Look in the *empty* tomb and ask Him to make all my hopes come to life.

See Him as a little boy in Nazareth. In Cana where He turned the water into wine and ask Him to change me, too, so I'll give joy to my world.

I won't forget to pray for you, Evelyn, Rebecca, Ronnie, Richard, Roberta—each by name, several times and several places.

I'll be home, Lord willing, by Dec. 15 or 16—.

Should I be called away I'll meet you at my permanent address: Palace of the King, New Jerusalem, Heaven.

All my love, Your husband, father and friend!
Oral (3 John 2).

WESTERN UNION

W. P. MARSHALL, PRESIDENT

CLASS OF SERVICE		SYMBOLS
This is a full-rate Telegram or Cablegram unless its deferred character is indicated by a suitable symbol above or preceding the address.	EX-1201	DL=Day Letter
		NL=Night Letter
		LT=Int'l Letter Telegram
		VLT=Int'l Victory Ltr.

The filing time shown in the date line on telegrams and day letters is STANDARD TIME at point of origin. Time of receipt is STANDARD TIME at point of destination

KB248

K.CDU142 32 PD INTL=CD JERUSALEMJORDAN VIA RCA 8 1510=

LT MRS ORAL ROBERTS= ARCHER AND BOSTON 2ND FL BEKINS BLDG

1638 SOUTH BOULDER TUL=

=EVELYN EVERYTHING I DREAMED ALMOST SPIRIT OF JESUS

HOVERS NEAR AM RECORDING MY FEELINGS PRAYED LAST NIGHT

GETHSOMANE NEW YORK MONDAY TUESDAY=

:ORAL ROBERTS=

:1638 GETHSOMANE=

THE COMPANY WILL APPRECIATE SUGGESTIONS FROM ITS PATRONS CONCERNING ITS SERVICE

NEWS OF TULSA
AND OKLAHOMA

SECTION 1—PART 2

TULSA

TULSA, OKLAHOMA, SUNDAY, JU

Total-Perso

THE PRESS

I have learned not to be overly impressed by the pros and cons of the press. As a general rule, people form their own opinions regardless of what they read. Usually, those who attend our crusades are impressed with what they see and hear, and make their own judgment. The press has been objective more times than not. One cannot ask for much more than that. However, in Tulsa, where we live and maintain our offices and the University, there is a noticeable difference. The press knows us and has been extremely objective and positive in their reporting. I admire their sense of fairness. In the final analysis, it is what we are that counts, not what others assess us to be.

—World Staff Photos by LeRoy Randall

ORU student Christine Fries, watches construction of seven-story dorm.

Learning Resources Center costs $4.5 million

MILWAUKEE SENTINEL

SATURDAY, NOVEMBER 8, 1958

MILLION SOULS FOR CHRIST'

oberts' Crusade Opens Tuesday in A

he Rev. Oral Roberts; evangelist minister, of Tulsa, Okla., will hold his 958 series of revival meetings in his "Million Souls for Christ" Crusade v. 11 through 16 in the Milwaukee Arena, under the sponsorship of the aukee Area Full Gospel Fellowship. The six-day meeting will be attended ding Full Gospel ministers from many states. Chairman of the ministers' mittee is the Rev. Lloyd Christiansen, 2320 East Park Place, Milwaukee, onsin. Rev. Christiansen is Pastor of the Lakeside Assembly of God ch in Milwaukee.

Admission to all Oral Roberts' services is free. Praye for the use of people attending the services who wish to ma for Oral Roberts' individual prayers, are given out at the There is no charge for these cards. No cards will be dist afternoon of the Crusade, Sunday, November 16.

Oral Roberts' 1958 series of Crusades consists of 16 m and one in Canada. They are held either in auditoriums a or in the famous giant, fireproof, 8-pole "tent cathedral"

hristiansen hairman; 30 Churches Aid

hirty churches in Milwau-a and neighboring communi-ies have undertaken the onsorship of the Oral Rob-r "Million Souls for Christ" usade which will open Tues-y.

Chairman of the campaign the Rev. Lloyd Christian-n, pastor of the Lakeside ssembly of God, in Milwau-e. He together with the Rev: hn Wannenmacher of the alvary Assembly, vice-chair-an of the campaign, have an-ounced that everything is in eadiness for the crusade which may draw upwards of 0,000 during the six days that e meetings will last.

This marks Roberts' second ppearance in Milwaukee.

Here are the churches spon-soring the crusade. From Mil-waukee are these: Assembly of God Churches: Bayview, Bethel Tabernacle, Calvary, Christ, Community, Grace, Full Gospel, Lakeside, Parklawn. In addi-tion these Milwaukee churches are sponsoring also; Church of the Open Bible, Faith Temple, Milwaukee Evangelistic Tem-ple, Milwaukee Foursquare

Christiansen   Wannenmacher

Church, Milwaukee Gospel Tabernacle and West Side Gos-pel Mission.

Others in Wisconsin are: First Assembly of God, Wau-kesha; Fond du Lac Assembly of God; Full Gospel Assembly, Menomonee Falls; Kenosha As-sembly of God, Kenosha; Keno-sha Foursquare Church, Lake-shore Tabernacle, Inc., Keno-sha; Mayville Gospel Chapel, Mayville; Peniel Tabernacle, Kenosha; Racine Assembly of God; South Milwaukee Assem-bly of God; Union Grove Gos-

A FAMILIAR SIGHT—ROBERTS WITH BIBLE IN HAND AT THE MIKE

Roberts' Work World Wide

In ten years the evangelistic ministry of Oral Roberts, the Ada, Oklahoma-born minis-ter's son, has snowballed into world-wide proportions.

Frail and stuttering as a boy, Oral Roberts found his own salvation at the age of 17. Now, at 40, he looks back to remember that his call to the full gospel ministry was the result of an almost un-believable recovery from tuber-culosis prayer has be her co healed as ma single in a s It i in a mate have and

other ministers in every man-ner of hall, auditorium and tent. He used his own "tent cathedral" for the first time in Durham, N. C., in 1948. His present tent, 400 feet by 200 feet, will seat 12,500.

Twelve Crusades so far this year in Corpus Christi, Texas; Miami, Fla.; Oklahoma City, Okla.; Huntington, W. Va.; Hempstead, N. Y.; Charleston, S. C.; Birmingham, Ala.; Syra-. N. Y.; Allentown, Pa.;

stories for children throughout the world; the distribution of complete films and tape re-cordings; and the publication of a magazine, ABUNDANT LIFE, has resulted in more converts to Christianity than the ministry of the 12 Apostles in their own lifetime.

Roberts has recently com-pleted his third "Million Souls for Christ" Crusade, having led more than one million per-sons to Christ during the 12-month period. He is now launching his fourth Crusade to take the

A STUDY IN CONCENTRATION

Evangelist Oral Roberts places both hands to his head as he pauses a moment in his

800 People Respond In Might
To Evangelist Roberts' Exhortations

By S. C. WARMAN

"God is a good God," evangelist Oral Roberts of Tulsa, Okla., shouted as he began speaking to an audi-ence of about 800 in the Ra-mada Inn dining room last night.

"Repeat after me, God is a good God," he said.

The audience echoed in great volume, "God is a goo God."

"Say it again urged. The audienc "Once more," he again the great ech a good God."

"Expect a new every day," he said a miracle from God he urged. And the repeated these exho too.

Everybody was stan list's message, but sa after this beginning.

Blind persons with canes, people in wheel and parents carrying sic dren lined up for faith ing, the thing Robert known for throughout ld.

ut the evangelist mad ial attempt to heal hem individually. Inst osed the meeting by pr for his audience as p.

verybody is sick in sor," he said. "None has ect body. We all have l. Lay hands on one an Everybody joined

and refused to have a collec-tion taken at the meeting.

He was the guest speaker for the Tucson Full Gospel Business Men's Fellowship In-ternational, a group that re-quires belief in the Pente-costal view of baptism by the Holy Spirit and of speaking in tongues.

His text came from Acts 1: 5-8, including the phrases, "but ye shall be baptised with the Holy Ghost not many days hence" and "but ye shall re-ceive power, after that the Holy Ghost is com

the religious practice of speak-ing in tongues.

The evangelist was th speaker when h had i

type of spiritual power was allowed to deteriorate among Christians, but has been com-ing back into popularity the past couple decades.

"All Jesus did," the evange-list said, "we are to do."

are built around a doctrine head . . . above added.

talking about," said, "is the the Holy Ghost de the personal is baptism, if Jesus by my ld heal people ne of them."

Roberts had arning: First, not to leave said in spite ominational rished mem-l church.

eaches me emotions. I when emo-ith truth," id, "When I am com-ut he said place for rs," "but I speak

a re-age, th rge, the God I am am ap-

Finns

Special to The Tribun

HELSINKI, Finland, J American Evangelist erts closed a four-day he termed the most su foreign crusade of his

He said he experienc criticism and that crowds among the largest of his

Sponsored by a group of tant Churches in Helsink Finland, Roberts spoke daily in a tent "cathedral the center of the city.

It was four large white joined into a single unit, se 12,500 persons.

"Every seat was taken many stood outside the te said Roberts. The tents we vided by Finnish churches.

THE EVENING SERVICE were in daylight, as the sun

$10,000 Dares Oral Roberts
To Prove Faith Healing

By JACK ROBERTS
Reporter of The Miami News

"It is against Oral Roberts' pol-icy to fight any man or any

vival in Miami Mr. Lewis aided a woman who brought charges

柏羅家道佈

敦請美國名佈道家羅柏牧師

市區中華基督教青年

地址：市

來吧！親愛的

請勿錯

看哪！神的權能

病痛退

時間：元旦

Ans

講題：耶穌

春新

信奮心興

...Scheduled
...red Lessons
...Roberts U

...iversity officials hope to ...pt. 7 with 600 under... ...s and a handful of grad... ...ologians, according to ad... advisor Charles Ramsey. ...tioned, however, that the ...has not yet filled its pro... ...quota and is still accepting ...ions.

...n evaluating an applica... ...e treat each student as an ...ual," Ramsey said. "We ...an autobiography and a ...s recommendation besides ...at the student's high ...grade average and College ...scores.

...hree-Phase Development

...e thing that inspires me ...ORU is that the university ...terested in more than just ...rain," Dr. Paul I. McClendon, ...ctor of learning resources. "Of course we are inter... ...in maintaining the very ...est academic standards. And ...are interested in the physical ...ects, or maintaining student ...alth. But the university also ...ognizes that the student has a ...l. We want to develop the total ...rson—mentally, physically and ...iritually."

...university will open with ...buildings, three of which are ...mplete now. The administration ...uilding and two two-story dormi... ...ories have been in use for several ...ears.

Buildings Described

The three buildings still under ...onstruction are one of three ...planned seven-story dorms, the Health Resources Building and the Learning Resources Center.

The Health Resources Building, a hexagonal, domed structure, houses the facilities to handle the physical end of ORU's "total student." A 25-meter swimming pool, a regulation size basketball court, an infirmary and various counseling services will be available in this physical education building.

Concern with student health is no new concept in university education, however. The unique educational approach at ORU centers in a complex computor matrix in the Learning Resources Center. This $4.5 million building is the core of the campus. Within its 192,000-square-foot interior are the campus library, classrooms, auditoriums, seminar rooms, specialized laboratories and the computor.

"The computor will have a profound effect on student's research," McClendon said. "If the student wants to study something he need only dial the correct digits on his student control panel. The message will go through a complex audio and video switching matrix to the source of needed materials.

Closed-Circuit TV

"The packet of materials the computor will select for the student would be impossible for him to compile by himself," McClendon continued. "It could include an appropriate five minutes of an hour film, a magazine article published the week before, tables from a professional journal and a portion of a lecture given on campus."

The possibility of seeing lecture films from classes missed particularly appealed to Mis... Although class attendanc... quired to avoid the ins... speaking to empty chair... camera, the films will ... able for excused absenc...

The playback device ... produce the materials on ... circuit television screen ... of earphones or in dor... classrooms and counselj...

This would enable instructors to use the prescribed study packets in lectures and guidance interviews.

Three classroom auditoriums are also housed in the six-floor lerning center. Each will seat 180. Opening the convertible partitions between the rooms will produce one 540-seat room. A screen at the front of each of the auditoriums is constructed to show films projected from the rea... rather than the front of th... screen. This innovation mea... that a film can be shown in normally lit room. Students ne... not struggle to take notes in t... darkness as in a conventio... projection room. Nor is it ne... sary that Braille versions of t... be passed out before the ... so that book references ca... made during slide presentati...

Another special facility o... Learning Resources Center ... performance analysis stud... any would-be dramatists ... the student body, McClendo... A student trying to w... a character interpretatio... give a performance and ... back immediately. The ac... to see and hear his own ... will have a head-start ... criticism.

The campus library, a... in the educational buil... include 60,000 volume... tember. McClendon exp... this is more books ... small universities ow... or 30 years of ope... were the books rando... The lists are those u... vard University and ... by Harvard and Mic... sities for establish... brary on new camp...

Freedom In T...

"I feel that the ... dom possible on th... be far greater th... at any state-sup...

THREE

...tball

...ive to Roberts

...s not set until ...nland are deep... ...5 per cent are ...theran Church.

...percentage of ...he converted ...who joined ...oice.

...eached their ...aling "lines" ...the services. ...sought Rob... ...cluded many ...n, Denmark, ...rmany, who ...gs these ...ians, Swiss ...the prayer ...mbers. ...ed Roberts ...as inter... ...line.

Berlin situation than the average American.

Prior to leaving for Finland, Roberts talked with President Kennedy at the White House. The president of Finland, vacationing away from Helsinki, invited Roberts to his summer home at the conclusion of the meeting.

However, he was unable toaccept, as he left Finland for the U.S. and a few days rest before launching a crusade at Dayton, Ohio, on Aug. 1.

A delegation of West German protestants asked Roberts to come to Germany, possibly Berlin, for a huge meeting in 1962.

"I am thrilled with this invitation, and will try and accept," Roberts daid.

His headquarters here said the evangelist will not return to Tulsa prior to his Dayton meeting.

Graham Will Talk at ORU Dedication

Formal dedication of Oral Roberts University will be held next spring with Dr. Billy Graham as the principal speaker.

Dr. Graham recently told Oral Roberts, president and founder of the school, that he would come to Tulsa for the event. The promise was made at the World Conference on Evangelism in Berlin, which both attended as delegates.

No date has been chosen, Mr. Roberts said. Other guests at the dedication will be state educational leaders, presidents of other universities, officials of the Department of Health, Education and Welfare, Dewey Bartlett, who will be governor, other high ranking state officials, members of the Legislature, Mayor Hewgley and city officials.

Mr. Roberts was introduced to the World Conference on Evangelism by Dr. Graham, and gave the group a summation of the proceedings. Dr. Graham said "Oral Roberts is a man I have come to love."

...elist Stirs ...Audience

...ARRY FERGUSON

...white canes, the ...

10,000 HEAR EVANGELIST

'We Were Cured' People Tell Oral Roberts Meeting

"R.D.M." STAFF REPORTER

A SMILING, 75-year-old woman told about 10,000 people at the Oral Roberts meeting in Johannesburg last night that she had been cured of cancer "at once" when Oral Roberts prayed for her at a meeting two years ago.

"I was given up by the doctors ...

...Roberts Praised Highly in Magazine Article

...th Tulsa evan... ...is something ...man thinking... ...hake" one up... ...noted for his ...great and near...

...day Evening Post ...Martin, in the first ...s in the Feb...

Yet, Martin writes, the evangelist emerged in his mind as quite a controversial ch... "loyally supported on hand and roundly den... the other."

FOR THE ARTIC... gathered information ...erts' various bases ... including Tulsa. ...he talked ...

persons. Most, although they did not agree at times with the evangelist's tactics, had great respect ...

trying to frighten people with hell and damnation, but rather one who disarmed them with kindness.

Martin was told there were plenty of detractors to Roberts, ...many leading Tulsans are ...e Roberts among ...

...Tulsa's prominent ...or a visit to the ...headquarters would ...ding the man's de... ...ving smaller in stat... ...New Yorker.

...TICLE tells of what ...be a rather unprom... ...e for Roberts when he ...en at 17 with what was ...as advanced tuber... ...both lungs.

...said while in Tulsa he ...ith the church editor of ...ahoma newspaper, who ...basically did not like ...but that he shouldn't be ...hort. The church editor ...Roberts' operations a busi... ...nd not a church. She said ...em concerning him would ...ppear on her newspaper's ...h page.

...e second in the two-part se... ...appears in March.

ARMED nightwatchmen have thrown a rigid security screen around Oral Roberts' "tent cathedral" following a mysterious fire last night.

Police believe a deliberate attempt was made to set fire to a huge American semi-trailer beside the tent.

...have been waiting a long time ...his—two years," she said. ...od is here to-night. I can feel ...can feel it," shouted Roberts, ...ng and waving his arms. ...owards the end of the meeting ...asked anyone who would con... ...e £5 to the expense of the ...

...burnt in three canvas covers in the trailer. Attendants told fire...

Oral was persecuted

'WE SHOULD BE ASHAMED' (says Dr. Benson)

MELBOURNE had "persecuted" American hot gospeller Oral Roberts during his stay here, Dr. Irving Benson said at the P.S.A. in Wesley Church yesterday.

"The intolerance and persecution shown toward this visiting ...

"Persecuted" ...

Why I Believe That God Works Through Me To Help Heal You

The Rev. Oral Roberts Explains His Famed Faith-Healing Ministry To Insider Readers

The Rev. Oral Roberts

By REV. ORAL ROBERTS

When people ask me: "Brother Roberts, what is your secret? How do you heal people?"—I have a standard answer.

I have no magical secret, and the Rev. Oral Roberts can't cure even the three-day measles.

There is only one Great Healer working at my crusades, and that is Almighty God.

But there is one thing that I can do.

I can help you find the point of contact at which your faith becomes strong enough so that your body is relieved of its afflictions.

"Point of contact with God" is the key phrase to my whole ministry. So let me begin by explaining it.

Your Faith

Suppose you have a quarter in your hand, and you want to buy a loaf of bread.

You are fully capable of buying the bread because you have the quarter, and the storekeeper has the bread waiting.

To get the storekeeper to release the bread, you must release the quarter to him.

...hat is a simple illustra... ...but the quarter repre... ...s your faith and the bread ...esents God's salvation for ...soul and the healing of ...body.

...point of contact is the ...of sending your faith to ...It is something tangible, ...hing you can do, and when ...it you release your faith ...God.

...e problem is how.

...as confronted with this ...n early in my ministry ...eople came before me for ...

...e said: "Brother Rob... ...have all the faith in ...orld." Yet they did not ...aled.

...ndered about this until ...t when a woman in the ...ine said to me: "Brother ...I have all the faith in ...ld."

...enly the answer came "That's your trouble, ...have it. You must re... ...," I told her.

...Not Enough

...not enough to have ...must be sent out of ...t, and directed toward ...

...lay my hands on you ...for your healing let ...

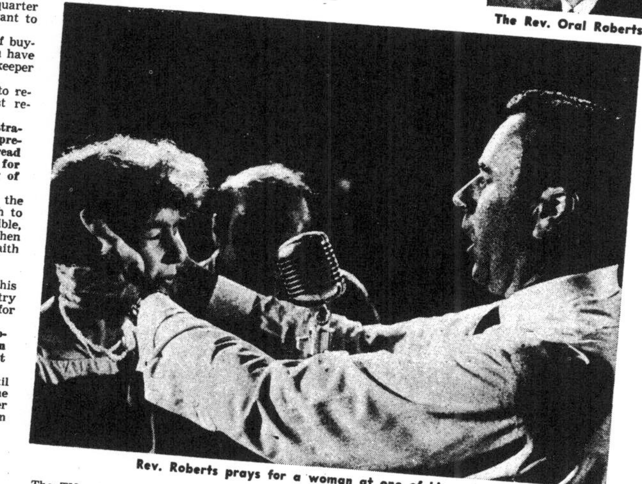

Rev. Roberts prays for a woman at one of his crusades.

The TV set, along with your faith, can be a sufficient link with God's power.

Definite Act

You can believe that God can heal your body, and you can firmly believe that healing is of God.

But until your believing becomes a definite single act your healing may never come.

All ...

symptoms, or relieved people of so-called psychosomatic illness—an ailment which exists only in the imagination despite certain physical symptoms.

False Hope?

They say I am giving false hope by "working people up" to the belief that they are cured by causing their ...

my parents had taught me: **"They shall lay hands on the sick, and they shall recover (Mark 16:18)."**

These vivid words struck my mind with great force. I focused my attention on God, and began to think that if only I could get to that meeting and have the evangelist put his hands on me and pray, God would heal me.

So I agreed to go, and made up my mind that when the ...

I saw no one for man... moments.

I saw nothing but the ligh... that engulfed my whole being.

I Was Cured!

My soul began to sing. A dee... fountain of power seemed t... break up within the bottom o... my being.

It came into my lungs and suddenly they were open and I could breathe! I could breathe deeply without wheezing and hemorrhaging!

When I came to my senses, I was on the platform, running, jumping and praising God.

I knew I was healed, for I had been bedfast for 163 days and had lost the power to walk alone.

But about a week later the reaction began to set in.

I was back home, knowing I was healed. But the Devil was whispering to me, "Why are you so weak? Why do you have to rest every afternoon?"

I asked my mother, "If I am healed, why am I so weak?"

She said, "Oral, it may be a year, maybe less, before you have all your strength back. **"The important thing is that the TB germs are dead.** "Now hold on to your healing —it came from God. Do you remember how it felt when the evangelist put his hands on you and prayed?"

And my mind went back to my point of contact. I could feel the minister's hands again, the power and glory and spirit of God that went through my lungs.

I remembered my point of contact and I stopped doubting.

That was in the spring. By early summer I was well again, preached my first sermon and won my first two souls to Christ.

Holding Belief

But what would have happened if I had not held on the point of contact through my mother's inspiration when the doubts set in?

Very likely I would have gone back to bed, and probably died.

In my subsequent ministry, this is the point I have tried to put across.

It is not enough to direct your faith to Jesus Christ at the crucial moment, although this is indeed critical.

You must continue to hold your belief in God's power to cure, until the last ravages of the disease have gone.

As you can probably tell, the basis of my entire ministry is summed up in my own cure and conversion back in 1935.

In summing up ...

Judging from the questions of visitors, Tulsa is well on its way to becoming the Oral capital of the world.

SEP 8 1965

Oral Roberts Will Speak At Full Gospel Conclave

The Full Gospel Business Mens Fellowship International will open its 10th anniversary regional convention Thursday in the Fresno Memorial Auditorium. The convention will run through next Saturday.

M. K. Stott, the president of the Fresno chapter of the FGBMFI, who is in charge of arrangements, said more than ...,200 persons are expected to attend.

The featured speaker during the three days will be ...vangelist Oral Roberts, who ...ill be making his first appearance in Fresno since ...58.

...Roberts, of Tulsa, Okla., ...l speak Saturday night at ...adult banquet, scheduled ...6:30 PM in the auditorium. ...outh banquet will be held ...he same time in the Hotel ...

Stott

Shakarian

tors of the FGBMFI. He was first elected to the post 10 years ago in Fresno when the first board of directors was chosen.

Others speaking will be James Brown, a Presbyterian pastor from Parkesburg, Pa., and Marvin Crow, a Baptist ...

Oral Roberts 'College' Opens; Tulsans Chee...

By Francis Thetford
Of the State Staff

TULSA — More than 500 persons of various religious faiths met Tuesday night to herald official opening of Tulsa's new Oral Roberts University.

"This is a great dream, unfolding before your eyes," Lee Braxton, president of the university's 51-member board of regents, said.

"I believe you are seeing history made here tonight," the Tulsan told the banquet audience.

Principal speaker was the Pentecostal evangelist for whom the new educational complex has been named — Oral Roberts.

"You've shown a certain amount of courage and ambition or you wouldn't be here," Roberts told some 300 students in the banquet audience.

"Here you can reach for excellence and find it," Roberts said. "In today's world you can not get through without it."

The evangelist said ...cal and mental deve... are only a part of th... swer to today's needs.

"The whole man will ...er be developed withou... training of the spirit," ...head of the $11 million li... ...al arts university said. S... ...it, mind and body must w... harmoniously together, R... erts added.

Actually, Friday will ma... the start of studies fo... university's first fre... class. Enrolment, limi... a shortage of dorm... space, was reported Tu... at 325 regular student... 30 graduate theology ...dents.

The $5 million T... Resou...

Oral Roberts Has Role in Berlin Event

Oral Roberts, Tulsa evangel... and president of Oral Roberts U... ...versity, will participate in ... World Congress on Evangelism ... Berlin, Germany Oct. 26 thro... Nov. 4.

The invitation to Mr. Ro... to be a panelist at the con... came from Dr. Carl F. H. ... editor of "Christianity T... chairman, at the suggest... Billy Graham, honorary ... man.

Mr. Roberts will sp... "Twentieth Century Evan... at the Nov. 2 meeting.

ON THE PANEL with ... be Dr. Harold John ... pastor of Park Stree... Boston; Rev. Efrain S... Puerto Rico, and Rev. ... of Switzerland.

Representatives of ... ...est and newest chur... ...be among ...

Big Future Is Seen for ORU's Theology School

By NELL JEAN BOGGS
Tribune Church Editor

"Give this theological school a decade and it not only will be the biggest in the Southwest, it will be the biggest in the country."

This was the opinion of one of Tulsa's leading ministers this week who was among some 185 persons attending a meeting ...

cussed briefly the school's goals, at the same time announcing a study course that will be open to the general public beginning Sept. 13.

Although requirements for the graduate school are quite specific, this is not so of the 18-week course to be held each Monday ...

Messiah," the first nine weeks and "A Harmony of the Gospels," the second nine weeks.

Dr. Corvin explains that the course will be divided into three parts—the first a lecture period, then a combination of lectures and audio visual, concluding with the people dividing into small ...

Dr. Corvin notes that discuss... leaders will serve more ... moderators to "pull out ... various views of people." T... dean admits to being quite excit... about the Monday night venture i... which enrolment is open until i... begins. He expects an enrolmen... in excess of 200.

God is moving in the hearts of men today,
*   Move with God,*
He is filling with His Spirit in a
*   glorious way, Move with God;*
Let your faith go, receive His gift,
Then you'll feel the flow of a surging
*   mighty river*
If you'll listen to His voice and then obey,
*   Move with God.*

Move, move, move, oh Move with God,
*   Glory, hallelujah,*
As true sons of faith have trod,
*   Glory, hallelujah,*
God is moving by His Spirit;
This is revival day,
So let us then determine in our hearts
*   the way God's moving, and*
*   Move with God.**

*From the song, Move with God, by *Vep Ellis*

THE SIXTIES
Moving with God

As we entered the sixties, a new president had been elected. In his inaugural address, he told Americans, "Ask not what your country can do for you; ask what you can do for your country." The new president was a vital man with a rare ability to communicate his spirit to people. His assassination in Dallas stunned America. People wept openly as they had done when Roosevelt died.

Vice-President Johnson became president and launched his "Great Society."

The economy of America was soaring. Technological advances were being hailed. It was confidently predicted that a man would be put on the moon in this decade.

The Supreme Court had made new rulings affecting civil rights. Marches of both white and black citizens began across the South. Riots broke out in northern cities. The press had a field day in sensational reporting.

Education took on a new aura of importance. College campuses were bursting at the seams.

However, there were ominous overtones, and thoughtful people were turning to the Bible to see where we were in history. Billy Graham's crusades reached an all-time peak in attendance. Our own crusades were packing the big tent and auditoriums virtually everywhere we went.

America was on the move; God was on the move. And we determined to move with God.

WORLD CRUSADE FOR SOULS

With my spirit throbbing with God's presence and my compassion aroused with His love, God thrust me forth into the world harvest again. We had begun the sixties with a trip to the Orient and the Iron Curtain countries. Now we were to begin a worldwide missionary and evangelistic crusade on five continents. God's command to me as a youth to take His healing power to my generation rang anew in my heart.

This would be the longest missionary and evangelistic trip I had ever undertaken, completely encircling the globe. Bob DeWeese, Tommy Tyson and Collins Steele accompanied me. It would require a book to tell you all that God did on that trip. Here are a few highlights from my diary:

WITH THE GYPSIES IN FRANCE

Since about 1950, the Gypsies have appeared to be strangely open to the Gospel. We drove through Marseilles, a city of almost a million people, to the Gypsy camp. Gypsies were there from France, Spain, Portugal,

We drove through Marseilles, a city of nearly a million people, to the Gypsy camp. What a sight! Gypsies were there from France, Spain, Portugal, Italy, Germany, Switzerland, Yugoslavia, Denmark, Belgium, Holland, Finland and other countries. Our tent was surrounded by a sea of trailers.

Italy, Germany, Switzerland, Yugoslavia, Denmark, Belgium, Holland, Finland and other countries. Dressed in colorful clothes, happy and spirited, they had come to their great annual meeting and to meet the American evangelists.

As we drove on the grounds, I saw the big white six-pole tent made in Finland. It was almost like driving up to our tent in America. Threading our way through the crowd, we entered the huge canvas cathedral. It was packed, with hundreds standing.

The Gypsies are a musical people. The platform was filled with their ministers and musicians, mostly with violins, guitars and bass violins. How they could sing and play! I didn't understand a world, but I *felt* plenty!

At last I was presented to preach and to pray for the people. I preached on Matthew 10:1-7, when Jesus imparted power to heal and told us to use it to heal the whole person. I ended with James 5:14-16; how it is the sick *person* who must call for divine help, and those who pray must direct his attention to the Lord who will raise *him* up.

The Lord anointed me and soon the great crowd and I were as one.

My French interpreter was excellent; he understood my phrases, gestures and purpose. Soon we both were in the swing of the message and I knew the people were being reached.

The response of the unsaved to the invitation was tremendous; they streamed forward and filled the front and part of the aisles. I noticed many young men under heavy conviction for sin. I love to see people accept Christ.

There was terrific excitement when the prayer line started. As long as the people wanted to come by, we let them — over two hours of laying on of hands. We saw miracles. One woman was so thrilled, I thought she would be raptured. She looked up once and, not knowing what else to do, threw a kiss to the Lord! Another young woman came by with heavy braces on her legs. After prayer she hobbled away, but stopped within 20 feet of us. She removed the braces, held them high over her head and walked away crying for joy. Instantly the crowd was on its feet praising the Lord.

Before our final services with the Gypsies, the ministers wanted to meet with us. This session was unusually fruitful. These pastors, carrying the responsibility of reaching thousands of Gypsy people in Europe, who have little or no education, were hungry for us to share with them. They drank in our words. The meeting ended with the laying on of hands for greater anointing for service. Over the years I've seen God use the ministry of the laying on of hands, and I am more convinced than ever that it is a key to the releasing of faith, a marvelous point of contact, and an instrument for the transmission of God's power.

I believe God has sparked revival among the Gypsies of Europe. It is an honor to have had a part in it.

HOLLAND

The closing service with the Gypsies left us excited and we were unable to relax, so we arrived in Holland after a rather sleepless night.

Holland is a most beautiful place — a low land of water, flowers, cows and hearty people. The City of Utrecht, founded during the days of the Roman Empire, was here when Jesus said: "Go ye into all the world and preach the gospel to every creature." I felt the same sense of urgency to preach as I did in Marseilles.

The Dutch people are big-bodied people with spirits to match. All day they came from throughout this nation of over 11-million people, by car, by chartered bus and by bicycle. I've never seen so many bicycles in my life. From children to grandparents, they ride bikes in Holland.

I delivered a message on "The Master Key to the Healing of Your Total Person." My interpreter was excellent. I was thrilled at the understanding of the great audience. During the invitation, hundreds came forward to accept Christ.

While I preached, Tommy Tyson was in the invalid room ministering faith to the people.

After a strenuous day, I began to tire while ministering in the prayer line. Bob and Tommy laid hands on many of the sick; this was something I had prayed for. In this way, the team ministers, instead of just one man, and we are able to help many more people.

The Saturday night service was something to behold. Thousands were present. The atmosphere was alive with the Holy Spirit. Never had Jesus anointed me more. When I asked the people to accept Christ as their personal Savior, hundreds upon hundreds came — serious men and women, fine young people — all wanting to know Jesus.

It reminded the team of our South Africa Crusade several years ago when 5,000 came forward to be saved in a single night.

NEW ZEALAND

I always get an odd feeling in the pit of my stomach upon entering a strange city or nation for the first time. What will God do here? Will the people respond or will they react? I do not always know which it will be. I've been on a height of glory in one city and struck with sudden persecution and near death in another. But always we go, for this is our mission.

New Zealand was among the places we ministered during our world crusade for souls. During a pastors seminar here, an Anglican priest said, "Reverend Roberts, in 1954 your literature fell into my hands. I was struggling spiritually. Through your books, Christ became real to me and alive in my heart. It was then I made the decision to become a priest and I have continued until this day. It is so good to meet the man God used to challenge me to know Christ."

While we were in New Zealand a plane was chartered to fly the team and the local committee to Rotorua for a crusade among the Maori tribesmen. We were met by several hundred friends singing, "Where the Healing Waters Flow." As we stepped on the ground the team was engulfed and we shook hands on all sides. What a welcome!

But this was nothing compared to the roaring welcome later in the auditorium where there was standing room only after the 4,800 seats were taken. Bob and Tommy ministered to this great audience at two o'clock. Later Tommy said, "Bob DeWeese was at his best. I've never seen him so anointed. People's hearts were stirred as the Word of God was expounded. Faith was in the air. You could feel the mighty presence of God."

At 6 p.m. one of the Maori brethren came to instruct me in the official proceedings to greet me at 7 p.m. in the auditorium. Here a Maori warrior would challenge me. This is an ancient rite of the tribe and was realistically carried out by a young man who played the part to the hilt. Followed by Bob and Tommy, I advanced slowly down the main aisle. The 50 performing Maoris were letting out bloodcurdling cries. The young warrior came toward us holding his ax high and twisting and contorting his body. A terrible look was on his face. Suddenly he stopped and placed a twig on the floor, let out another bloodcurdling cry, threw the ax toward my feet, then picked it up and dared us to move.

The great crowd sat breathless as the warrior repeated this maneuver. Turning to Bob, I whispered, "My heart is in my throat. Where's yours?" He replied, "Same place."

I was motioned to advance. Near the front the warrior rejoined the larger Maori warrior group. Then, leaping high in the air, clicking his feet together, throwing out his tongue, and walling his eyes, he let out another scream. The entire group took up the ceremony and brought it to a stirring climax. The crowd loved it and (I think) we did too.

We felt honored, as this was the Maori welcome given to the Queen of England and other world dignitaries.

In spite of the thrill of the moment and their welcome, my heart was heavy. I knew that most of them had been exposed to Christianity but were not really converted to Jesus Christ. There was so much I wanted to share in the brief weekend we had with them. I poured out my soul about Jesus Christ and His willingness to make men whole in body, mind and soul. They listened raptly. When I finished, I drove a hard bargain, as a pastor said later. I told them that if they had never accepted Christ and were willing from their hearts to repent and change inside, I would pray with them. "Make no mistake about this call," I said. "You cannot deceive God. He knows your heart and your way of life. If you come forward, you are saying to this audience and to your people that you are a sinner and are taking Christ as your personal Savior."

None of us knew what to expect, but in a matter of minutes hundreds jammed every aisle and completely filled the front.

The pastors were visibly moved; I felt like crying aloud. The Maori people had been touched and their response was overwhelming. About 15 percent of the crowd of some 6,000 accepted Christ. One couple told of a spell cast over them by Maori witch doctors and how, at last, through Christ they were free.

The healing service that followed was an absolute explosion, spiritually speaking. I began praying with the invalids. The first miracle was the healing of a woman on steel crutches. I saw she was being healed and said, "Rise and walk, in the name of Jesus of Nazareth!" And let me tell you, she did! The Maoris saw her take her first faltering steps, then break into a fast, steady walk. They rejoiced, clapping their hands and glorifying God.

The crusade among the Maoris touched me to the depths of my soul and gave me a burning desire to go to the peoples of this world—in person—more often and with more of the power of God in my ministry.

If our partners in America could have been with us, they would have seen what their faithfulness has done to win souls!

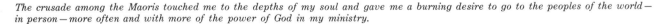

The crusade among the Maoris touched me to the depths of my soul and gave me a burning desire to go to the peoples of the world—in person—more often and with more of the power of God in my ministry.

Norman Armstrong (background) directs our overseas office in Australia. We also have branch offices in New Zealand, South India, South Africa, Great Britain and Canada.

AUSTRALIA

Nine years had passed since that never-to-be-forgotten night when a mob was permitted to break up our crusade in Australia. The questions passing through our minds were: *What will happen this time? Will we see any results from our crusades in Sydney and Melbourne? What will the press undertake to do against us this visit?*

Imagine our delight to hear our cab driver say, "Brother Roberts, I was converted to Christ in your crusade here nine years ago. God really picked me up from the gutter. I was an alcoholic and virtually bankrupt. I came to the meetings out of curiosity and there my entire family was saved. Now I am prospering and in nine years I've not wanted a drink. I've not missed a church service and I am daily witnessing for my Lord."

He took our breath away. "Tell us more," we said.

"My ulcers were healed, my life was cleaned up, and I'm a happy man today."

It was like that for three days; person after person came to us saying, "I was saved," or "I was healed," or "My family was delivered," or "I'm preaching now."

A little woman, a dwarf with a crooked back, straightened up the last night in Melbourne. Now she walks and drives a car! It was a real joy to shake her hand. A doctor said, "My wife and I found Christ in your crusade and have attended church every Sunday for nine years."

Our team ministered two days to the pastors who had come from throughout Australia, and on the first night, to 720 of our dear partners. If ever we have seen the power of God poured out and gratefully received, it was in these services.

"You men have encouraged us," we were told by their leaders. "We believe great things are ahead."

We wondered how the masses of India knew who we were and why we came. The missionaries told us, "In India, the two best-known names in Christendom are Billy Graham and Oral Roberts. Your literature is read by tens of thousands and many have also seen your films." Never had we seen such a demonstration of the effectiveness of literature.

INDIA

At last, another part of my 1958 vision for the healing of the nations came true. I had seen India in a vision and heard a brown-skinned man say, "Oral Roberts, when are you coming to us with the Words of Life?" Since the vision, my heart had ached to visit India and to minister to the teeming millions there. I felt God with us in the big jet as we streaked across the blue sky.

We arrived in riot-torn India amid newspaper headlines telling of rioting students wrecking trains, killing police and halting traffic. It made our United States newspaper accounts of race relations seem tame in comparison. The Prime Minister issued a special call to the nation. Still the rioting raged.

In Trivandrum we learned that thousands were on buses, trains and planes on their way to our crusade. Many of them were delayed because of the riots. It seems no great crusade had been held in this city, the capital of an area only 60 miles across, where some 15 million Indians are jammed together at the rate of 1,000 per square mile.

In the former palace of the Maharaja, 1,000 pastors from all North and South India were seated on the floor and filled every window and open door. A sea of brown faces and white-clad bodies looked up at us when we arrived.

In my message I told of my vision of 1958 and I said, "I am here in answer to that call for help. This is a moment ordained of God; therefore, we can expect miracles and can see God work as never before."

In the evening we went to the stadium and found about 15,000 waiting for us. "How did all these people know of us?" I asked the leaders.

"In India, the two best-known names in Christendom are Billy Graham and Oral Roberts," they replied. "Your literature is read by tens of thousands. They have seen your films. By Sunday," they said, "there will be 50,000 present."

The people thronged the stadium for each service and by Sunday, there were approximately 50,000 present. We had prayed about how to conduct the prayer line. How could three men minister effectively to thousands of sick people. We could exhaust ourselves and scarcely pray for a tenth of those wanting and desperately needing the Lord's touch. God spoke to my heart to have the thousand pastors take up stations in the audience. As I directed them from the pulpit and prayed, they were to lay hands on each one. I told the audience what to expect and hoped for the best. It happened! A wave of prayer swept up like roaring waters; the power of God came like a shock of electricity. It was so strong on the platform, I cried out

I cannot describe the burden on my heart as I preached to these Indians — 50,000 in one service.

This young Indian holds his crutches high as a witness to the healing he received. Because of the thousands who asked for prayer, we asked 1,000 national pastors and missionaries to assist us in the prayer lines. Many of the people received miracles of healing.

to Bob and Tommy, "It's as if we'll be translated."

At four o'clock we accepted an urgent call to pray for the Maharani, mother of the Maharaja of Kerala State, whose beautiful palace is only five minutes from the hotel. The tutor, a cultured Anglican woman, came for us and on the way told us many things of the royal family.

The Maharani graciously received us and served us tea. Then she told of her need of healing. She had not been able to receive any help for a condition now spreading over her hand, arm and shoulder. Although a high caste Hindu, she said she was a strong believer in healing. She believed Jesus was a good man, but not divine.

I gave her my personal testimony and witness of Christ. When I touched her, I did so calling upon the name of Jesus of Nazareth. The power of the Lord filled the room as much as I've ever known before. It was surprising, in a way, to find such faith in this woman who was not a Christian. I discerned that she had been seeking God and was open to the Lord. So often the need of healing does this in the human spirit. I told her that her healing would come from within her, that it was she I was praying for, not merely her hand and arm.

At that time the Maharaja came in. He was a man of slightly less than medium

height, obviously an intellectual, and a man with a kingly bearing. He profusely thanked us for coming. He was glad, he said, to meet a man who had great faith and in whom God's gifts were working; and, he said, he was honored to have such a man in his home.

"Have you met Christ?" I asked.

"No, I have not," he replied. "I am a Hindu."

"Would you like to have a contact with Christ?"

"I am afraid not. You see, I have been taught from childhood that duty is paramount — my duty is to my gods. No, I am not open to Christ."

"Sir," I said, "I have prayed that Christ will reveal Himself to you, and I have assurance that He will. When He does, I know you will have an open mind to receive Him."

"Oh, yes," he answered, "I will keep my mind open."

Before we left India, a missionary remarked, "The best thing about your crusade to us missionaries is for the first time, the pastors from all the areas have sat together in unity and prayed together to win souls. I've prayed for this for 40 years. Now, I am seeing it in your visit here. The pastors are stirred to go to villages which have not heard the Gospel."

The committee chairman termed the results of our crusade: "A new day for us in India," and we knew he meant it.

In the early sixties, I traveled to the Orient and behind the Iron Curtain. I went to visit and to pray with the Protestant leaders. There is relative religious freedom in Poland. In Warsaw, Poland, I was permitted to speak in a small chapel—400 people packed the room. One night, 30 accepted Christ. In this service, I shared with these Polish Christians the message of healing through the Communion.

In Formosa, Bob DeWeese and I were privileged to have an audience with Generalissimo and Mme. Chiang Kai-shek. I told them of my gratitude for their welcome and for their great influence for Christ on the island. It is this influence which is chiefly responsible for the freedom of religion in Formosa.

Moscow, Russia. Russian people are taught there is no God; but, I found those who still believe! I am expecting a great revival to break out in that country.

More than 300 national pastors and missionaries gathered in Atami (near Tokyo), Japan, for a workers' conference. I believe these dedicated workers hold the key to the evangelization of Japan.

THERE IS NO SHORTCUT
TO A MIRACLE

In the crusades, we have found there is no shortcut to a miracle. A crusade is more than a tent meeting or a revival in an auditorium. A crusade is a personal experience. It is a personal encounter with a living, loving Jesus who wants to make YOU whole.

The preaching and the hearing of the Word of God is the most important part of the entire crusade. I know that when I preach I must be anointed by the Holy Spirit. Since 1947 when I vowed never to enter the pulpit without first feeling God's anointing upon me, I have been tested many times. I remember in a Philadelphia Crusade, the time came to leave my room and go to the auditorium. I had been in prayer for more than two hours but I did not feel God's presence within. It was time for me to be announced to the crusade audience, but I refused to leave my room. I said, "Lord, I cannot heal, I cannot save, I cannot do anything to deliver those people waiting for me until You energize my being with the power of the Holy Spirit. I will not go until You anoint me." I actually read Luke 4:18 to God where Jesus said, "The Spirit of the Lord is upon me, because he hath anointed me to preach the gospel to the poor; he hath sent me to heal . . . ."

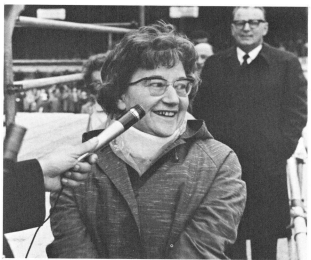

"Lord," I said, "if Jesus Christ Himself had to have Your Spirit upon Him and to be anointed before He could preach and heal, how much more must I be permeated by Your anointing Spirit?"

I had no more than said those words, when the Spirit of the Lord came upon me. I hurried to the auditorium. When I stood before the people, I was not concerned with the atmosphere. I had God's Spirit in my heart and the people could sense it.

In 1960 I sensed a greater anointing of the Holy Spirit than ever before. A new moving of the Spirit in the world was revealed to me during our crusade in Dayton, Ohio. As I entered the pulpit to preach on the opening night, the Lord said, "Preach on the baptism with the Holy Spirit tonight." Discarding the message I had prepared, I spoke on the Holy Spirit. The team knew I sometimes used this

The Wales Crusade. "Medical doctors had done all they could do but I suffered constant and terrible pain. I had been told my disease was incurable and would only get worse. I had no hope in this life or the next. I went to the crusade crippled by cervical spondylosis, sclerosis and arthritis. When I was prayed for, God instantly healed me. Not only was I physically healed, but I was spiritually reborn. I went home, took off my collar and spinal support, and slept like a baby. I awoke to a brand-new life." — Doreen Tyrrell, Llandaff, South Wales

In spite of rain, the crowds packed the Newport Athletic Stadium in Wales. The singing of these Welsh people blessed our hearts. I may have to go to Heaven to hear singing that is more beautiful and exhilarating. And, never have I found a people who were more hungry for God.

message later in the crusade but never in the opening service.

I shared with the Dayton audience how the baptism with the Holy Spirit opened my mind and spirit to a ministry of the supernatural. I stated that the healing ministry, as I knew it, was through people filled with the Holy Spirit. There was a quickening of the audience and large response to the invitation to accept Christ. During the crusade Bob DeWeese and the sponsoring pastors laid hands on those seeking the baptism with the Holy Spirit. Several hundred received the Baptism and spoke in tongues. In many

instances the moment they laid hands on the individual, he would be immediately filled and able to speak in a new tongue of prayer and praise to God. The healing miracles in this crusade were also tremendous.

After the Dayton Crusade I began a restudy of the Holy Spirit and the value of tongues, as well as the nine gifts of the Spirit. During this crusade I saw that I should help make others aware of this power — that it comes only through the baptism with the Holy Spirit and constantly living in the Spirit.

After several months of prayer and

intensive study, I wrote a book on the Holy Spirit. More than a hundred thousand people wrote for a copy. Thousands have received the infilling of the Holy Spirit since reading this book. One woman merely glanced through the book and found her heart quickened with a hunger for the infilling. She received the Baptism and spoke in tongues easily and naturally. She became a transformed woman, one who could witness boldly for Christ. Before, her walk with the Lord was more or less confined to her home and her church. She has since become a regent of ORU and is one of the most anointed and dynamic Christians I know.

I wish it were possible for you to go with me into the invalid section of our crusades just one night. You would see from 50 to 70 desperate people, some in wheelchairs and some on stretchers, others held in the arms of loved ones.

I remember as I began this ministry how difficult I found it was to give hope to these people. When they come to our meetings, most of them have been given up by medical science. They have been given up by loved ones and, worst of all, they have given up themselves. There is no response from them.

It was a real spiritual struggle through the years to get these people to stand up on the inside. But, in the past few months something has been happening in our invalid section. The message of "standing up on the inside" has been getting through. In a crusade in Daytona Beach, we saw 30 people rise from wheelchairs.

I recall in a crusade in Stockton, California, I had prayed in the invalid section for several nights without much success. It was heartbreaking. One evening I decided to do something drastic. As I stood before this group I demanded, "Listen, why are you here?" Several of them indicated they were there to be healed. "You certainly don't act like it," I replied.

Some recoiled as if I had struck them. "When Jesus Christ was upon the earth," I said, "He often said to an invalid, 'Rise, take up thy bed and walk.' He did not engage in long prayers or use many words. He simply gave his command of faith and the people responded or did not respond. You must make up your mind that tonight is the night that you can be helped. But you must do some-

Vep Ellis, our crusade minister of music, has been used of God to set to music many of the concepts of this ministry.

In the past few months, something has been happening in our invalid tent. The message of "standing up on the inside" has been getting through. When we come into the tent now there is movement. There is life and hope. The inner man is rising. The Holy Spirit is strengthening the invalids on the inside.

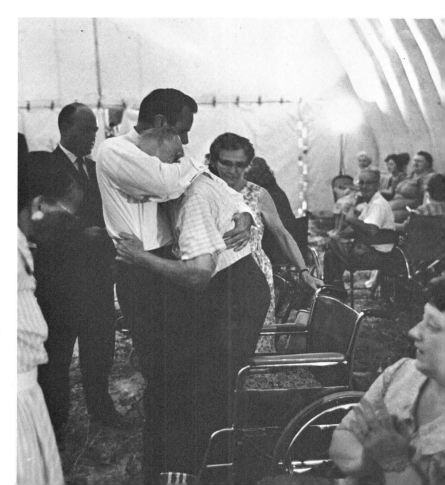

thing about it yourself. Some of you, as I have touched you, have not made any change inside. You look at me as if I could heal you. Well, I tell you, I cannot heal anyone. If your faith is in me, you are doomed to disappointment. If your faith is in Christ, there is hope."

I sensed they were beginning to understand. I said, "I am coming to you now, not in my name nor in my strength, but in the name of Jesus Christ and through His power. I am going to touch you in the name of the Lord and give you the same command of faith that Jesus gave, 'Take up thy bed and walk.' This is all I am going to do. Are you ready?"

I asked four of the sponsoring pastors to go with me. I said, "Pray as I pray." By this time there was an expectancy present. When we finished praying for all of the invalids, thirteen of them had risen from wheelchairs and stretchers. Some of them leaped and shouted for joy. Others cried like children. We saw more results in that brief period than we had in all of the previous evenings of the crusade.

"This proves one thing," I told the pastors, "God wants to heal but we must do our part and the people must do their part. There is no shortcut to a miracle."

Philadelphia, Pennsylvania. A crusade is more than a revival in an auditorium or tent. It is a personal experience. It is a personal encounter with a living, loving Jesus who wants to make YOU whole.

Stockton, California. God wants to heal but we must do our part and the people must do their part. We can pray in faith but the sick person must "take up his bed"—he must respond in faith.

Kokomo, Indiana. I think one reason that people love to come into the prayer line is because it is a positive place. It is a place where God's power is. It is a place where people are believing.

A NEW BREAKTHROUGH IN EVANGELISM

In order to take the message of deliverance to my generation, I knew I must do it not only through our world outreaches and myself personally but also through the minds, hearts and hands of others. I felt the time had come to undertake by faith the greatest and most far-reaching step of all — our *eighth* world outreach — the Oral Roberts University. Through it we would see a new breakthrough in evangelism.

God had spoken and said, "You are to build the school out of the same ingredient I used when I made the earth — nothing." That is exactly where we started — with nothing. We had no special funds, no faculty, no students and little promise of obtaining any.

We did have a ministry based on the ministry of Jesus Christ, a ministry that was much deeper and stronger than a casual hearing or seeing would suggest.

Although the details would take years to work out, even then we envisioned a tri-purpose university. We looked forward to a School of Evangelism, where seminars could be held for laymen, partners, ministers, etc.; (2) a fully accredited liberal arts university for our youth, and (3) an accredited Graduate School of Theology for the training of ministers and workers in the power of the charismatic move of the Holy Spirit.

The School of Evangelism was the first phase completed. It officially opened in January 1963, and consists of seminars and special conferences for several days at a time. The School of Evangelism has ministered to more than 5,000 pastors, evangelists, teachers, youth and partners from throughout the world! They have returned to their churches, businesses, homes and schools with a new understanding of the Holy Spirit and of God's miracle power. Their influence has already multiplied our ministry many times over. Today the School of Evangelism continues to be a vital part of our ministry.

Through the years, I have watched the young people in our crusades. I have seen thousands of them won to Christ and many of

This big earth-moving machine is symbolic of the sixties for we have been moving with God in building Oral Roberts University — a construction job which seems to have no end.

them healed. I have seen in them the potential of evangelizing the world. I knew it would take youth — but trained youth, youth on fire with the Holy Spirit.

The Lord revealed to me that the University would be an evangelistic tool in the hands of the Holy Spirit. We were to recruit faculty members with proper academic training that made them equal to the task and thoroughly acceptable to the educational world. We desired faculty who would be open to, and hungering for, a new breakthrough in Christian education that only the Holy Spirit could give. They would put their Christian witness first and would not be afraid to dream of a mighty breakthrough and to expect it in their generation. The Lord held this before me as a challenge. It was evident He wanted a university that would measure up academically and at the same time be directed by the Holy Spirit.

When the ABUNDANT LIFE Magazine announced plans for Oral Roberts University, it captured the attention of our partners everywhere. Many wrote of their joy at this new venture and hoped it would be built soon enough for their children to attend. We had scarcely started construction when a partner in her seventies drove up from Texas with her grandson who had just finished high school and asked, "Can I get him in the University today?"

A PROPHECY CONCERNING MY MINISTRY

During the International Ministers Seminar in 1963, one of the European ministers called me aside and gave me a prophecy. I knew it was from the Lord for it confirmed what God had already revealed to me. The minister said, "You have been raised up in this generation to fulfill a task that only you can realize. God has focused your faith on a divine project related to a renewal of healing power in the Church. He wants you to maintain the position in leadership in which He has set you. If you will be faithful, He will make you big enough for the task."

He spoke of the connection of the evangelistic crusades with ORU, "When you return from the crusades, say to the students, 'We have seen God in action'. The crusades are a live demonstration of God in action to deliver people. Keep the crusades and the University related. Remember that the Prophet Elisha built a school. The school never took away from Elisha's ministry but rather increased it."

The International Seminar was host to spiritually influential people from 56 countries of the world. They came with heavy burdens for their people. Many left with a new power in their lives to meet those problems — through the release of the Holy Spirit in their lives.

Our first youth seminar gave us a preview of what the University would be like when it opened in September 1965. The buoyancy and vibrancy of these young inquiring minds made the campus come alive. It was a thrill to share with them individually as well as to minister to them in group sessions.

The School of Evangelism has become a "spiritual workshop" where groups of ministers, youth leaders, laymen and partners meet in seminars to share fresh truths from God. Already more than 5,000 have attended. This is a typical Bible study session in one of our partners seminars.

OUR PERSONAL COMMITMENT TO ORU

Evelyn and I continued on the love offering as a means of personal support until about 1960. At that time, we felt directed to go on a set salary. We decided to give what we had saved over the years to ORU. After much prayer I discussed this with my team, then with the Board of Trustees of our Evangelistic Association.

Dr. R. O. Corvin tactfully questioned me, was I doing this because of criticism? Was I feeling pressure from critics? Or, was I being moved from within?

I said that I was taking this step as one of faith and through it demonstrate to myself and to the world that my financial income did not in any way determine the course of my personal ministry. I had vowed never to touch the gold or the glory. It is a good feeling to know the vow has been scrupulously kept. I wanted to leave a testimony that what I had done in the ministry was not due to either a small or a large income. I did it because I loved God and people.

With everyone understanding the decision, I went on a set salary. I have been just as happy as I was before. I have learned that a Christian has to change, not in principle but in method. It is not always easy to do but it is absolutely necessary for growth in Christ.

My vow to accept no private gift given in connection with my prayers for people still holds. This limits my income in a tangible way but our God is not limited and in His limitlessness, I fully trust. I know that God is a good God. I further know God is *always* a good God.

I was highly honored in 1963 to be named "Outstanding American Indian" of the year. I am of Cherokee descent and have a burden on my heart for the salvation of my people. One of our Eight World Outreaches is our ministry to the American Indians.

The award was given at the American Indian Exposition in Anadarko, Oklahoma. Although it was not a religious occasion, I was able to give my testimony to the people. These young boys were "all dressed up" for the event.

January 27, 1962. ORU was officially founded and officers and regents were installed. I was grateful for the prayers of these regents as I accepted the responsibilities of president. (Left to Right: Nick Timko, Demos Shakarian, myself, Evelyn, Henry Krause, Dr. John Barton and Oscar Moore.)

Dr. Raymond Corvin and I were both converted as teenagers under the ministry of my father, E. M. Roberts. Today, Dr. Corvin is serving as Dean of our Graduate School of Theology.

An architect's drawing of the Oral Roberts University as it will appear when completed. Eight buildings are completed: Learning Resources Center, Health Resources Center, Timko-Barton Building, Shakarian Hall, Braxton Hall, the power plant, a high-rise dormitory and the Prayer Tower.

THE MIRACLE OF THE CHARISMA AT ORU

Ordinarily it takes many years to establish a university. A building program of large magnitude must be undertaken, an endowment program initiated, a curriculum formed, a faculty of major scholars secured and students recruited. The challenges and problems inherent in such an undertaking are breathtaking. It is good that I did not know all that was involved for it might have staggered my faith. All I knew was God had commanded it to be done. We began as if it were no greater challenge than any of our other world outreaches. The University seemed to go up so quickly that it surprised the entire nation. Both religious and educational leaders were astonished. At first, there was much skepticism.

It reminded me of 1947, when I began this ministry with the announcement that I had been raised up by God to take His healing power to my generation. Some people who had known me all my life said, "We will give this idea a year — two years at the most — then it will fade." Some ignored it altogether. But God began to anoint us with His Spirit and soon the ministry was moving across the nation. First it was a trickle, then a stream, then a flood! It was God's doing and it was wonderful in our eyes.

When the first three buildings of the University were completed on the new campus in 1963, the news spread far and wide. Those who came to attend the seminars told the story of what they saw and of the larger plans for the future we had shared with them.

Within a few months, we had heard from prospective faculty members. They had heard we were building a university based on the concepts of our ministry, in which each faculty member would be filled with the Holy Spirit, and where the most advanced teaching aids and methods would be used. One wrote, "God has given a breakthrough in healing and soul-saving. I believe

He is raising up ORU for a new breakthrough in Christian education that only the Holy Spirit can give. I want to join you in this step of faith. I too am dreaming of a mighty breakthrough . . . and am expecting it in this generation." His statement, "a mighty breakthrough in this generation," witnessed to my heart. God had told me in the beginning that the ministry was to be taken to this generation. This statement from a prospective faculty member served to confirm what I have already begun to feel about a special work God wanted to do. It was apparent the University had a much broader purpose than an academic opportunity. It would be in the forefront of the breakthrough.

God works through men. I believed then, and I believe even more strongly today, that the right men, anointed by the Holy Spirit, can lead the University into one of the most powerful forces for God in this generation and in future generations, until Christ returns.

Through the years I have seen a pattern emerge among the type of people God has drawn to our ministry. Because it is a ministry to meet needs, it has appealed to people who have needs and know they have needs. More than one-half of our crusade audience is composed of people over fifty years of age. However, there are many teenagers and children who also attend. You can look at those coming forward to accept Christ and you see people of all ages, from the youngest to the oldest. In any invitation you will see scores of young high school and college youth as well as older men and women.

A professor, a Ph. D., who was filled with the Holy Spirit, said to me, "Brother Roberts, what will happen to all these people and to your ministry when you are gone? This may be a painful thought, but it has to be faced."

I replied, "Has the Lord given you a thought on this?"

"Yes, I believe He has," he said, "and it is this: Success without a successor is failure."

I then asked, "Since God has begun to raise up the University, how do you feel it will fit into the ministry?"

"Under God it can be a successor that will

It is my privilege, on occasion, to share with groups of students what God is doing in the crusades. It is inspiring to hear from them how God is moving on the campus, filling with His Spirit and changing young lives.

The Graduate School of Theology is dedicated to the task of preparing young people of all denominations for their chosen vocations, academically, culturally and spiritually. It is dedicated to academic excellence in the glow of the Spirit-filled life.

continue sending forth young people throughout the world," he answered.

This professor is now a member of our faculty and is part of the breakthrough that we envisioned.

People who are filled with the Holy Spirit in the Pentecostal dimension have suffered much for their testimony and faithfulness. This has caused them to withdraw into groups where they have become rather exclusive. They have been so thrilled with what God is doing through them in witnessing to this generation that they have partially ignored education. In a way, they have been a little afraid of education. One of the re-sults has been that thousands of young people growing up among them, or who were attracted to a faith that emphasized the gifts of the Spirit, have been neglected as far as their education is concerned.

The young people attending our crusades have responded to the ministry. I have seen more than three hundred accepting Christ in a single service. As many as 700 have attended one of our youth seminars. After they are won to Christ or are healed of some affliction, what then? Where do they go?

Today, with or without their parents' guidance, they are going off to college. The whole nation is changing in this respect.

The eternal flame is set permanently in the middle of a black marble fountain under the arches of the Learning Resources Center. It represents the Light of the World, Jesus of Nazareth.

Language students listen and respond to as many as ten different programs simultaneously in this modern language lab. Either they or Dr. Tibor Barteky (shown in the foreground) may record their responses by means of tape decks in each individual student booth.

Education is in the forefront. We are told that soon fifty percent of the nation's population will be under twenty-five years of age. By 1970 more than seven million young people will be in college.

The Church is not keeping pace with the world population which is said to be growing at the rate of 65 million a year. Just to keep up with the increase, it is indicated that 57,000 people a day would have to accept Christ as their Savior. These startling figures do not take into account millions of young people who are now saved.

The military might of the nations of the world rides on the shoulders of their young men. Many of the brightest witnesses for Christ in Bible days were young men and women. Some of the Apostles, it is believed, were barely out of their teens. Our Savior was only 33 when He died!

A little sign, "Expect a Miracle," hangs on the wall of the campus dining room. It captures a lot of attention when visitors pass through. To us it is more than an attention-getter. *Expect a Miracle* is more than a slogan. It is a way of life. Many wonders and miracles have happened through this ministry, through the University, and must continue to happen. There is no other way that

God's work can be fully done.

What does a sign, *Expect a Miracle*, have to do with a college campus. Colleges usually think and act empirically. Reason is the hard core of their program. Miracles are ruled out as being unrelated to the pursuit of knowledge. Supernaturalism has been set aside as antiquated and irrelevant in a sophisticated age. That may be acceptable to those who do not believe the Bible is the Word of God or that Christ is the divine Son of God. To us, God's healing power gave us our life, His will became the purpose for our existence, and His Gospel, the vehicle of our expression and outreach. We stand on the power of Christ's Gospel. We believe the Gospel should be the motivating force behind the University.

A professor from an ivy league school visited the campus recently. He was impressed with the buildings, the educational media, and the competence of the faculty and the students. He startled me by saying, "What a shame that this is a Christian campus."

"Why do you say that," I exclaimed. "What kind of school do you think it should be?"

"It should be a secular campus," he replied.

When I saw that he was serious, I said,

The ever-broadening reaches of learning necessitate a university equipped with all the latest learning devices. ORU provides these ... and much more.

Part of each student's and faculty member's activities include regular workouts in the Health Resources Center.

The University opened in September 1965 with 300 students. This year there are 546 students on campus. Next fall, September 1967, we anticipate an enrollment of 700. Our goal is to have facilities for 3,000 students.

"I thought in a Christian nation where people believe in God and the Bible, this is the kind of campus that is urgently needed at this critical hour."

"I don't believe in the Bible," he said. "It is unfortunate for so beautiful a campus to be in your hands." This was putting it rather bluntly but it was the way he felt. He spent nearly an hour trying to convince me that

ORU should become a secular campus. "In that way you can be free to study truth and be a real university," he concluded.

"On the contrary," I replied, "I believe that truth can be pursued here with the fullest freedom of all. Christ is truth. To know Him is the beginning of truth. With Him as our guide, we can explore truth wherever we find it and be free to apply it

to meet the needs and problems of mankind."

"I wish you well," he said.

Looking around the campus I told him, "Each of these buildings was constructed or is being constructed through the prayers, faith and sacrifices of people who know God. They have dreamed of a university where their children could study in an atmosphere where Christ is preeminent, and where through Him they could break through limitations and bring forth new knowledge and wisdom for the human race. Here you will see exciting things happening in the fields of knowledge — things that can happen only on such a campus."

"Perhaps," he said. Then he smiled, "If I should ever come to believe in God, I would like to teach here." Once again he looked across the campus and said, "How beautiful!"

"When he left I told an associate who had given him the tour of the campus, "If it is as beautiful as he says, then I am glad it is in the hands of the Holy Spirit. There will be many efforts to separate it from its

ORU students utilizing the comfortable lounge furniture on the fourth floor of the Learning Resources Center. These book shelves now contain 50,000 volumes, arranged according to the Library of Congress classification scheme. The library has space for 500,000 volumes.

The electronic marvels of tomorrow are available today to help ORU students forge the educational tools they will need for the work of a lifetime.

purpose. Pray God it shall always belong to Him."

As we have carefully and prayerfully considered it, there were four difficulties in developing ORU as God intended. First, a Spirit-filled faculty had to be secured.

The educational world knows how difficult it is to secure a faculty with any degree of competence. When you add to this the deep dimension of the Holy Spirit, the difficulty is increased.

When he heard of our commitment to a Spirit-filled faculty, a leading churchman said, "Oral, in our church colleges we used to have a requirement that faculty members should be dedicated Christians. Now we just ask that they won't fight us. If this has been our experience, how can you expect to secure faculty who are not only Christians but are filled with the Holy Spirit as they were in the New Testament. I don't believe you can do it."

"We knew it would not be easy when we started," I replied. "It was not easy for Christ to surround Himself with 12 dedicated men. Even one of them became a betrayer. But when Christ rose from the dead and met with His disciples, He told them they were to be baptized with the Holy Spirit not many days hence. He instructed them to tarry until they had received this gift of power from on high. The second chapter of Acts records: "They were all filled with the Holy Ghost and spoke with other tongues as the Spirit gave utterance." These Spirit-filled followers of Christ became teachers, preachers, business leaders, etc. If the Lord could start His work in this way, we believe He will give us ability to find men and women who want it continued in the same way through the University."

While recognizing the difficulties, I firmly believe this is the course Christ wants us to take.

Another leading churchman said, "It's well and good to be filled with the Holy Spirit, but why insist on tongues?"

"The infilling of the Holy Spirit and tongues went together in the New Testament," I replied. "They should go together today. God has a purpose in doing it this way. He is our Guide and we must follow Him."

The 200-foot Prayer Tower is the spiritual heart of the University. Here the Abundant Life Prayer Group is on duty 24 hours a day. The crowning tongues of flame ever burn to symbolize the Holy Spirit.

"Do you require every faculty member to speak in tongues?" he asked.

"We don't approach it from that angle even as they did not in the Book of Acts."

"What do you mean?" he asked.

"Jesus told His disciples to receive the gift of the Holy Spirit. He did not emphasize speaking in tongues. Peter, in preaching to the house of Cornelius, did not stress speaking in tongues. Paul's message to the Ephesian brethren on receiving the baptism with the Holy Spirit did not refer to tongues. But when the disciples at Pentecost received the baptism with the Holy Spirit as Jesus had commanded, they spoke with tongues. Cornelius and his group received the same gift and they spoke with tongues as the disciples did at Pentecost. The brethren at Ephesus received the Holy Spirit and spoke with tongues when Paul prayed for them. In other words, when the infilling of the Holy Spirit came, they were given the ability to speak in tongues. As Paul later taught in I Corinthians 14, tongues are to edify the inner man. As long as there remains a need for a Christian to edify himself, there will be a need for speaking to God "in the spirit," or in tongues.

"We do not emphasize speaking in tongues any more than the early Church did. We simply accept it as a part of the infilling to be used primarily in our private devotions to God. We find the same release and therapy that the early Christians found. It is a valid and valuable help to us in being more effective in prayer and in praise to God. In holding to this position we are neither adding to nor taking from the Scriptures; it is a natural part of our Christian experience."

He listened patiently, then said, "I can't see it, especially in a university."

"Whatever a follower of Christ seeks to

The first seven-story high-rise dormitory accommodates 600 students. The appointments in the dormitory make provisions for a counselor on each floor, a social hall, a recreational hall and a meditation chapel.

do or to become, he should have the same close union with Christ whether he is a farmer, a businessman, a doctor, a preacher, or a university professor," I explained. "He needs the infilling of the Holy Spirit."

"But tongues . . . ?"

"Which came first in the Book of Acts, the baptism with the Holy Spirit or tongues?" I asked.

"The baptism with the Holy Spirit comes first."

"And tongues followed?"

"Yes."

"It's the same today. We don't seek tongues. We don't put a premium on tongues. Our emphasis is on the infilling of the Holy Spirit and all that comes with it."

"Just what do you hope to gain by this? Won't it make you exclusive?"

I replied, "Surely there should be at least one private university in the world where the instructors are filled with the Holy Spirit and speak in tongues. Have those without this experience brought forth a mighty breakthrough in Christian education? I believe God wants us to see what He will do through a university that is staffed by people who want the same Holy Spirit infilling and accompanying gifts as in the early Church. That is the way Christ started it. Perhaps He wants at least one place that will follow this pattern. At any rate, why not wait to judge, until after the University has been in operation long enough to see its results?"

We were touring the campus as this discussion was carried on. Suddenly he asked, "What about your students? Do all of them have the Holy Spirit and speak with tongues?"

"As far as I know, some do and some don't."

"It's not a requirement for enrollment?"

"No, it is not. The requirement we make of our students is to be open to all God's truth, to all His gifts."

"This includes the gift of tongues?"

I said, "I am glad you mentioned the gift of tongues." We make a distinction between the baptism with the Holy Spirit and a gift of tongues."

"You don't feel they are the same?"

"In our experience, it is not. It was not in the Book of Acts nor in I Corinthians 12

TULSA DAILY WORLD

"Oklahoma's Greatest Newspaper"
EUGENE LORTON
1869-1949

Page 6   Monday, January 23, 1967

Published Every Weekday Morning and Sunday by World Publishing Company
BYRON V. BOONE, *Pres. and Publisher;*
L. W. McFETRIDGE, V-Pres.;   ROBERT E. LORTON, Sec.-Treas.;
SID STEEN, *Executive Editor*   WALTER BISCUP, *Editor of Editorial Page*
PHIL DESSAUER, *Associate Editor*   N. G. HENTHORNE, JR., *Associate Editor*

BIBLE THOUGHT
The Lord shall guide thee continually.—Isa. 58:11

Good News For ORU

IT'S A FINE compliment to ORAL ROBERTS University to be accredited by the State Regents For Higher Education so soon after its founding.

The accreditation means that students at ORU will be able to transfer their credits to other colleges and universities in Oklahoma. This in effect recognizes ORAL ROBERTS U as an equal among the State's higher schools—in only its second year of operation.

Also in the mill is similar recognition by the important North Central Accreditation Agency, which sent an inspection team to the campus in southeast Tulsa last fall. Once this is received, the school's standing will be advanced beyond the borders of Oklahoma.

ORU has a beautiful campus and striking physical facilities; that much is apparent to anyone who pays it a visit. But a university's plant is only one facet of its development; its true worth comes from the kind of education it provides.

This is why the accreditation by the State Regents—in President ORAL ROBERTS' words, a "vote of confidence"—is so vital and encouraging to all who are interested in our community's newest center of higher learning.

and 14. As you know, in the Book of Acts, when Jesus, Peter and Paul spoke of the gift of the Holy Spirit, they referred to the baptism with the Holy Spirit or the infilling of the Holy Spirit. When this infilling was received, tongues were included. Later, Paul referred to nine gifts of the Holy Spirit. These are: gift of the word of wisdom, gift of the word of knowledge, gift of faith, gifts of healing, gift of working of miracles, gift of prophecy, gift of discerning of spirits, gift of divers kinds of tongues, and gift of interpretation of tongues. Paul enumerates these in I Corinthians 12:4-11 and explains how they are set among God's people. He states that each gift is for profit or to meet needs, and each gift is given by the Holy Spirit as He sovereignly wills. In our view, these gifts include the gift of tongues in one's private devotions to edify himself. There has to be a special or a critical need and then, the Holy Spirit may manifest through an individual Christian one or more of these nine gifts. The Spirit may see an urgent need for wisdom and He would empower a child of God to speak a special word of wisdom. Or, there may be an urgent need of healing and the Spirit would empower one with a gift of healing to bring recovery. Or, there may

The Board of Regents consists of outstanding leaders, professional men and women from across the nation and is the governing board of the University. Lee Braxton is chairman.

The ORU choir contributes meaningfully to the spiritual life on campus and often sings in seminars and conferences.

be a need of deeper insight and perception concerning a specific situation that has become critical, and the Spirit would enable one to give a word of knowledge or a prophecy that would shed light on the situation or confirm some particular way God is moving. There may be an urgent need in a group of believers to be edified and the Spirit would manifest a gift of tongues followed by a gift of interpretation to reveal God's message and make it plain.

"Manifestation of one of the nine gifts is a different thing than receiving the baptism with the Holy Spirit. And this is the way it is practiced in our ministry and at the University."

My friend replied, "I had not seen it in that light before. In other words, when you speak in tongues in your private devotions, it is really your spirit giving expression to prayer and to praise. This is a power you have because of the infilling of the Holy Spirit. And this is not the same as when a gift of tongues is given. A gift of tongues is given sovereignly to meet a special need, say in a group. Is that right?"

"Precisely."

He said, "On your campus, if I were with an instructor or students in prayer, I might hear them praying and praising God both in English and in tongues?"

76

"Yes. But they would not be praying in tongues because you were there, even as they would not be necessarily praying in English because you were there. What they do, they do naturally and as Paul says, 'In decency and in order.'"

"A gift of tongues then may be manifested when they are together?"

"Yes, that's right," I said, "God might manifest a gift of tongues; He might not. It would depend upon the need, in the same way that a gift of wisdom or a gift of healing would be exercised if there were a special need."

"What does this have to do with the professor's teaching?"

"It has to do with the professor's walk with Christ in the overall sense," I explained. It helps him to pray better, to praise God more effectively. It edifies his inner man. It opens him up more readily and completely to the Holy Spirit's work in himself and to the supernatural. He doesn't speak in tongues in his class nor do the students. In class they are busy about their tasks. But when they speak to God either silently or audibly, they may pray in tongues. As I said, it is primarily done in our private devotions."

I am repeating our conversation to set the record straight. You may come on campus and be there several days without hearing anyone speak in tongues, either as part of his private devotions or as a gift of tongues which God may sovereignly manifest in behalf of some collective need. Or, you may hear it the first day you arrive. You would see, however, that it is a natural expression of a heart that is seeking God, or that is magnifying the name of the Lord. It is not manifested as a badge of exclusiveness nor as a token of pride. It is the sincere desire of the heart as the Spirit gives utterance.

My friend pointed to a girl we were about to pass. "Does she have the infilling of the Holy Spirit and speak with tongues?"

"I don't know. Let's stop and ask her."

After asking the girl her name and address, I said, "What church are you a member of?"

"Presbyterian."

"Do you have the Holy Spirit?"

"Yes."

Mamma and Papa Roberts, now 82 and 86. I owe a debt to them that can never be repaid.

When one of our boys was injured and carried off the court, God miraculously healed him after prayer. In two minutes he was back in the game, causing the coach of the other team to say, "We can battle your basketball team, but a miracle we can't contend with."

My friend said, "When did you receive this?"

"Since coming here."

"Why did you desire it?"

"Here at ORU you are brought face to face with all truth in the Bible such as prayer, dedication, giving, service to others, Holy Communion, honesty, unselfishness, the gifts of the Spirit, fruits of the Spirit, etc. I saw and felt something here that made me hungry to be a better Christian. I learned that I could ask for the Holy Spirit and, if I asked in faith, I would receive. One day I was studying the Book of Acts and was led to ask for the gift of the Holy Spirit. At first I was surprised that I received so quickly and naturally. My whole being was flooded with God's power and love. It was wonderful!"

"Did you speak with tongues?"

I laughed and said to him, "See, you are the one bringing this up. I did not. She did not. We talk about receiving the Holy Spirit and the power and love that come, and people want to know about tongues."

The student asked, "I don't mind answering that, President Roberts. Yes, I spoke with tongues. When the Holy Spirit filled me, I lifted my voice to praise the Lord and all of a sudden I was speaking new words I had never learned before. Now every day I pray in tongues when I talk to the Lord."

"Do you feel this is helping you?" my friend asked her.

I wondered what she would say, how she would answer. I had seen her on campus and met her along with all the others but had not heard she had been baptized with the Holy Spirit. Of course, this is constantly going on and we are never surprised.

She said, "I feel a release inside. My spirit opens up to the Lord. I feel quieter, more calm, more sure of God's presence. This has helped me in my studies, especially when I face a hard test. After studying and before I take an examination, I spend a few moments praying in tongues and it's wonderful how the Lord helps me and gives me assurance that I will remember what I have studied."

"Thank you, I appreciate your sharing this with me," my friend said, and we went on.

He asked to meet other students and we selected six more at random as we walked over the campus. An amazing thing happened. The first girl and the six boys and girls we stopped and talked to later had the infilling of the Holy Spirit either before or after coming to ORU, and all seven were Presbyterians! My friend knew we had not planned it this way. He exclaimed, "Imagine that, all of them Presbyterians!"

Of the 546 students, I think only 27 are

The School of Evangelism of the Oral Roberts University officially opened January 16, 1963, with a ministers seminar. More than 350 ministers and their wives, representing 11 different groups from 27 states, made up this first class.

The Health Resources Center is more than a gym for sports and physical exercise. It is the hub of teaching the anatomy of health. Facilities include a regulation basketball court and a junior olympic-size swimming pool.

Presbyterians. Each one has the Holy Spirit and speaks in tongues in his private devotions, and each is articulate in sharing its benefits. This is almost a miracle!

I smiled, "It sort of shakes one up, doesn't it?"

"It certainly does. It's something I want to think about."

Wherever I travel and meet Christian leaders, or when they visit the campus, the issue of tongues arises. I have no desire to push it or be silent. When I am asked, I answer. We have no pat or set answers. It makes little difference who you talk with, or what their denominational preference is — Pentecostal, Baptist, Methodist, Episcopal, Presbyterian or some other, all of us are hungering and thirsting for more of the Holy Spirit, for it is the Holy Spirit who speaks of Christ who is the Lord of our lives.

There has been controversy, and perhaps it is not yet finished, concerning the baptism with the Holy Spirit on our campus. This may be a good thing. Sometime, somewhere, Christians must face up to the relevance and efficacy of this dynamic experience and what it can do to help us find truth and walk in its light, and to bring greater power and love and to share these with all men.

Some earnest Christian leaders whom we love and respect may feel dismayed over our stand. Perhaps our stand should be questioned so that we may be sure it is the one God has ordained that we take. It may be that our stand is not for every campus. We seek to impose on none. But as for us and our house, we will follow the way God is leading us. We hope to make a valid and lasting contribution to God's people everywhere.

The Learning Resources Center has been called by the Ford Foundation "one of the most creative facilities on the American campus today." In this unique six-story learning complex the student has at his disposal a highly sophisticated information storage and retrieval system, employing the latest in electronic achievement and computer technology.

A DAY OF TRIUMPH

On September 7, 1965, we welcomed our first freshman class of 300 to ORU. Concurrently the Graduate School of Theology opened with 30 students. In my opening address, I challenged the students:

"In the history of the human family, there has been only one completely whole man. This was Jesus of Nazareth. Our concept of the whole man is derived from His life and from the example He left us. Combining what we know about Him with the most modern techniques of higher education, we have brought into being this new University and through it, we reach for *wholeness*.

"While others are reaching for a ride to the moon, you will reach for a whole life.

"ORU is a daring new concept in higher education. It was planned from the beginning to innovate change in all three basic aspects of your being — the intellectual, the physical and the spiritual.

"There's an education here for your mind, for without the development of your intellect you cannot be a complete person.

"There's an education here for your body, for that, too, is essential to your development as a whole person. Jesus is our great example. He personified health and vitality.

"There is a unique opportunity here for an education or development of your inner man, for the most important part of you is your spirit.

"The world doesn't need more college students to wave flags, carry placards, halt traffic, and riot against law and order. What our civilization needs is that you will make your spiritual development a normal part of your education and your life.

"*You can emerge as the world's most wanted college graduates.* A healthy body that you know how to take care of, a trained and disciplined mind that never settles for less than excellence, governed by an invincible spirit of integrity, inspired by a personal relationship with a living God, and driven by an irresistible desire to be a whole man to make a troubled world whole again!"

This second year, 546 students are enrolled — including freshmen, sophomores, juniors and graduate students in the School of Theology. Next fall we anticipate 700 students with an increase each year thereafter of 200 until we reach our maximum capacity of approximately 3,000. We will also have our first graduation next year.

October 31, 1965. I led 300 modern-day "Gideons" in a march of faith to light an Eternal Flame heralding a new day in Christian higher education, and symbolizing man's quest for wholeness. These "Gideons" each pledged $10,000 or a total of $3 million to build the Learning Resources Center.

GRADUATE SCHOOL OF THEOLOGY

The Seminary, the first graduate school of the University, is also located on the new campus of the Oral Roberts University. Dr. R. O. Corvin is the Dean.

We have invited outstanding church leaders and educators to assist in laying a foundation for a Seminary program that will soundly, effectively, and dynamically represent the historic Gospel of Christ and the charismatic operation of the Holy Spirit.

Although our students receive their theological education on our campus, we urge them to minister within their own church organizations. The Seminary is servant to the whole Church. We cherish Christian unity without exacting church uniformity.

I AM REMINDED: THIS IS GOD'S UNIVERSITY

We have just launched an additional building program at ORU. This will include a men's dormitory which is already under construction, a student union, a performing arts building, and a Chapel seating 2,000. In seeking to raise funds for this tremendous undertaking, God has taught me another lesson.

Recently I approached a philanthropic foundation, asking them to pledge one-half the price of one of the buildings. I told them that I would ask my partners to give the other half. Just when it seemed that the request would be granted, it was turned down by the board of directors.

When I told Evelyn, she said, "Honey, you ought to know by now that the Lord is not going to let any one organization give you a big amount of money. You're not building this University, the Lord is building it. He's going to build it the way He wants to. I believe He is going to have it built on $10 here and $25 there, $100 here and $500 there, with maybe a few larger gifts.

"Oral, we have partners who have a part in our ministry and a part in this University because we have allowed them to give little amounts of money. They feel a part of it and

Dr. John D. Messick, executive vice-president of ORU, gave the address at the dedication of the Learning Resources Center. Dr. Messick is the chief designer of the academic program of the University.

you can't take that away from them. Our partners want to have a part in this and God wants them to have a part. Honey, this is not your University. It is God's University. I had this feeling two weeks ago, but I didn't want to tell you because I knew it would just knock the faith out of you. I just have a feeling that the Lord is not going to let you depend on any human."

"Evelyn," I replied, "I believe you're right. God has used this to remind me that I must depend on Him. We must not depend on men for our supply. God is our supply and we have to depend on Him."

In the history of the human family, there has been only one completely whole man. This was Jesus of Nazareth. Our concept of the whole man is derived from His life and example. Combining what we know about Christ and the most modern techniques of higher education, we have established a university with a new concept; and through it, we reach for wholeness.

CAN A UNIVERSITY
AND EVANGELISM BE COMBINED?

When I first discussed plans for the University with my Team, they were excited and thrilled. They shared this dream with me. But they saw it as a project of the future. They were not prepared, as I was, for the *timing* or the *manner* in which I wanted to establish it.

When I announced, "Now is the time," it took them by surprise which soon turned to consternation and fear. "Oral," they said, "We know when you start something, you put everything you have into it. If you are going to start the school now, we feel we ought to have an official meeting with you on it."

I shall never forget what happened the day we met in the Abundant Life office. I was caught off guard when I walked into the room where the Team and staff leaders were waiting for me. There were no smiles, no camaraderie. "Sit down, Oral, we must get something off our minds," they said.

Immediately I sensed something was wrong. "Men, what's the matter?"

Different ones began to speak or to ask questions in the most frank way. They knew they could do this with me since that is the way we had always dealt with each other. For awhile it went beyond frankness. There was genuine concern that I was about to wreck the evangelism work we had been doing. The conversation went like this:

"We know God has told you to build a school. We want to know is this the time?"

"If I know anything at all about God's time for anything I have been led to do, then this is the time."

"Why haven't you kept us informed so we would have had things in more readiness to begin?"

"We've talked about it many times."

"Not in a definite way we haven't."

"Men, what is the real trouble here? Why are you all upset like this? You know I don't move unless I am led of God and every time I have moved in obedience in the past, we have met with success."

"That's just the problem, are you moving in God's will, in God's time?"

By this time the room was filled with tenseness. I looked around and thought: *Are these my own men.* The questions began again.

"Oral, do you know the financial condition of the ministry? What are you going to use for money to build the University? How do we know the partners will go with us on this venture?"

I told them, "We will start this new venture like we have every other one we have undertaken — with nothing on hand."

"But Oral, how long can we continue operating like this? Especially, when what you are proposing could become the largest expenditure of all?"

"Men, in my view, that is not the question at all. The question is does God want us to build the school. If God has said to build it, then we have to proceed as if we had all the money we need."

Manford Engel, the executive vice-president, a close friend who had been with me when this ministry started in 1947, had been delegated to be chief spokesman for the group. Now he took the lead.

"Oral," he said, "We have to know exactly where we stand with you."

"Manford, you stand where you have always stood; you stand with me in world evangelism," I answered.

"Let me put it plainly — how can a university and evangelism be harmonized? Will our partners understand? Will this bring confusion to everyone concerned?" he questioned.

"We will be all right if we do it as God has said. We'll take it step by step."

"Do you really believe the University will be a success?"

"Yes I do, definitely. Someday it will be our largest outreach for souls."

Manford looked around at the group, then said, "Oral, these men left good jobs to come with your evangelistic ministry. Many have been here for ten years or more. You have had the best years of their lives. It would be extremely difficult for some of them to return to industry or the professions and find a position equal to the one they have here. Our question is, if you build the University and it goes over as you dream it will, what will happen to all your men?"

These men had wives and children, and a future to face. What right did I have to expose them to a future that they might not fit into as they did in the current way the ministry was being carried on? They had given the ministry their best, now were they to be set aside and see their jobs swept away?

It dawned on me that I needed to do some real communicating. I should have already done this for I knew Scripture taught that the leader usually gets the message of God first before the workers do (Psalms 103:7). God had given me the revelation of the University, also the way it should be built. He had done this before revealing it to the men who were charged with carrying on the functions of the work. What I had to do was to make clear to them exactly the way God had shown me, and how they would be expected to fit into the picture. They were only reacting to fear of the unknown. Once they understood it as I did, they would be as enthusiastic as I was.

"Here is what God has shown me," I explained. "Our regular evangelistic ministry will be carried on in the same way as in the past — crusades, radio and television, literature, Hebrew Bibles, Indian work, Abundant Life Prayer Group, overseas crusades — everything. We will build the University and begin with a School of Evangelism consisting of seminars for ministers, laymen and youth. We will add to this the Liberal Arts Division and the Graduate School of Theology for those who desire higher training. We will notify our partners of each step we take.

"The University will grow and become a center for world evangelism. From it will go thousands of highly trained young men and women to carry the Gospel to the uttermost parts of the earth.

"You are men I depend on because you are filled with the Holy Spirit. You have been loyal and faithful. You have been closer to me than my own brothers. With you at my side, we can move forward and build the University as God has ordained. You can help see that it is spiritual, anointed, evangelistic, as well as academically strong and excellent. You will help secure the staff, the faculty, and the students.

Then, looking around at the group, I said to them, "Let us unite and rise up and build for the Lord!"

When I had finished I was on my feet, I was churning inside and my spirit was reaching out to these beloved men. Manford let out a gurgling sound and burst into tears. Lee Braxton sat with tears streaming down his cheeks. Bob DeWeese was broken up. R. O. Corvin was both smiling and crying. I don't know how it happened, but in moments 12 men were on their feet and we were embracing each other and praising God!

I was relieved and thrilled that those men were willing to take a step of faith with me. However, I realized there might still be questions in their minds as to how this would actually work out. Others had tried before to combine a university and evangelism and had failed. Would ORU? Our crusade in Rio de Janiero, Brazil, in August 1966, answered this question.

November, 1966. Faith, the force that began this University, is called upon once more as we break ground for this men's dormitory. God has already supplied one-third of the funds for it and we are trusting Him for the rest. This building will be similar to our present seven-story dormitory.

Maracanazinho Auditorium, Rio de Janerio, Brazil. I told the people, "This is your hour. God is here now to save you." It grew quiet and still in the big stadium. People were weighing these words. The Holy Spirit was driving the message deep into their hearts. When the invitation was given, two-thirds of the audience stood to their feet. This was the greatest sight I have seen in my entire ministry.

BRAZIL

This was our first crusade in Latin America. It was also the first time that we had taken a group of students along as part of the team. Tommy Tyson and Bob DeWeese, my associate evangelists, accompanied me.

We were deeply moved to be in the great land of Brazil. It has one-half the population of South America and is wide open to the Gospel and in great need of a deliverance revival. I was told that Brazil is second only to Haiti in the practice of spiritism and voodooism, with something like one-third of its people indulging, causing thousands to be bound by demon power.

I wish my partners could have been there. How proud you would have been of your "Investments." I wish you could have seen these students in action as they ministered by song and testimony. You would have been deeply moved, as I was, by their praying for the sick and entering in wholeheartedly and carrying their share of the load as team members.

One morning Tommy and I went to observe the students in a street service as they gave out literature and prayed for the people. They gathered in an open marketplace and started singing "God Is A Good God" and other songs in the Portuguese language. People soon surrounded them. The students testified and gave a word from the Bible. Then they asked the people who had needs to come for the laying on of hands.

I stood on the outskirts beholding these young people with their clean, eager faces and hearing their testimonies — first in English, then in Portuguese. I felt their passion for souls and their compassion to meet needs.

People were healed right there in the marketplace.

Later, at the hotel, one of the students said, "Oh, I feel an ache in my soul for these people. We've got to do more, to love these people and minister to their needs."

From the beginning of the crusade, the students ministered with us in the prayer line. I prayed till I grew weary then I asked them to take over. I sat nearby, praying for God to open the hearts of the people to their prayers. As they prayed for a boy of about 14, who was nearly blind, he cried to his parents, "I can see! I can see!" I rushed over to the boy, and found it was a miracle. I examined the thick glasses he had been wearing. Now, he saw clearly without them. He was hugging his parents and proclaiming to them the miracle of his sight. The students were in rapture. This was the first major miracle in which they had participated by prayer in a great mass meeting.

One particular miracle of deliverance made a lasting impression on the students.

There is much demon power in Brazil, and many of these captive souls were present in the crusade. A woman came through the prayer line writhing and twisting. Her eyes seemed glazed, and her whole being was one contortion after another. Two of the students stood to my right and had been assisting me from time to time, laying on hands and praying for the people. When I saw this woman coming, the Spirit of the Lord swept over me in a most powerful way and I intercepted her as she approached the students.

Suddenly the demon seized her vocal cords and began to speak. My interpreter told me what she was saying, "I will not come out of her. You can't force me to come out. I will not let you cast me out." Her husband tried to control her. She would come near me, then fall back with these words coming out of her mouth over and over. This was the most terrible case of demon possession we had encountered in a long time. Putting my hand on her head and holding her firmly, I began calling the demon out in the name of Jesus of Nazareth. As I spoke the demon would cry, "No, no, I will not leave." Twice I commanded it and the second time the demon, with the speed of lightning, struck her as with a heavy club. Her feet flew from under her, and she hit the floor as if she had been thrown by a giant. The sound of her body hitting the floor carried through the vast auditorium. A gasp rose from the crowd. Those in the healing line nearby fell back, some crying out in fear.

"Leave her alone, she's all right now." Instantly her face was suffused in light, her eyes opened wide and she cried, "Gloria a Deus!" (Glory to God). She rose to her feet transformed by our Lord Jesus, a new creature in Him.

The students who saw the entire miracle, later spoke in awe of this demonstration of God's power. One said, "I needed to see this, for in my Christian experience I have had no opportunity to witness this type of miracle. Only with this type of power can I ever help people like this and I intend to have it, God being my helper."

There were three types of miracles that dominated the healing line: the healing of blindness, the healing of crippled limbs, and the casting out of demons. There were many other types healed, but these seemed to be the ones most often healed. It mattered not if I did the praying, or if Bob or Tommy did, or if the students did. As when Jesus was in the house where the paralyzed man was let down through the roof, "The power of the Lord was present to heal."

The students shared with us one of the greatest altar calls of our ministry. It happened in the closing rally. I had just finished a straight-forward salvation message to a packed house of 17,500 people. Then I asked Bob to give the invitation. "You are not here by accident," he told the audience. "God wants above all to save your soul. He asks you to turn away from your sins, to earnestly repent, and receive Jesus Christ as your eternal Lord and Savior. This is your hour, and God is here now to save you."

A few hundred stood. Then, like a pebble thrown into the water with waves spreading in all directions, it seemed as if three-fourths of the people rose to their feet. Their voices became a mighty roar as they repeated the prayer, "Lord, be merciful to me a sinner...."

The students and I, standing back a few feet from Brother DeWeese, could not hold back the tears.

These were sincere people, caught up in the move of the Spirit of God, and they knew it was a spirit different from the one that had been holding them in bondage.

Even now I can feel the impact on my own soul as I look back and see this vast crowd standing, as it were, "on tiptoe" to reach Christ and find salvation. I love the healings, for I am called to take God's healing power to my generation; but to see souls saved is our higher objective, and to witness a scene like this is to remember it all the days of my life. I knew I would not forget nor would our students.

More than 7,000 were in the prayer line that followed. We prayed more than three hours without a pause, using three complete lines, will all the students participating.

I moved constantly among the students to whisper encouragement, to give a word of direction. When I would hear a student say, "Touch him, Lord," I would tell that student, "Don't say, 'Touch him, Lord', say 'Heal him, Lord'. The Lord wants to do more than touch, He wants to deliver completely." They appreciated this. At other times I would say, "Don't touch them too hard but get a firm grasp." Then, "Careful now, let the Spirit discern through you, watch for demon influence over some of these people." Then, "Don't get your eyes on the disease, keep your mind on Christ."

Every now and then one would turn and whisper, "Thank you, Brother Roberts." Later they all said, "This is the first time we've been actually involved with this many needy people, and the first time someone has told us how to minister. We are grateful."

I appreciated having a group young enough to be eager for Christ, humble enough to take advice, loving Christ enough to lay hands on the suffering, and willing enough to spend over three hours with me in the healing lines that afternoon.

At last the long lines ended, the last one was prayed for, and we stood for the final benediction. A wave of joy mingled with sadness swept over us and the audience. We longed to stay another week. But our next crusade in America was only a week away. The team was exhausted and we had a long all-night flight to New York.

A friend once said to me, "Success without a successor is failure." As I watched and guided these students ministering with me in Brazil, I knew that God would provide successors from among the students of ORU to carry on the evangelistic outreach of this ministry.

We lifted our hearts and hands and prayed for Brazil, for South America, and for the vast harvest fields of souls in all the world.

Back in Tulsa when I shared the Brazil Crusade report with the men, they rejoiced. I saw on their faces that their questions of a few years before had been answered with finality.

One of the men said, "I feel awed that this ministry to the whole world did not come into its fullness until the University came into being—now there is a means. Some may have felt that there was less emphasis on the evangelistic ministry and worldwide outreach during the time it has taken to build ORU. However, through the University, we are training students to be effective and to reach out to do a job better than Oral Roberts could have done alone. The University is a retreat to train, to implement, and to give direction to students who will take this message of deliverance around the world."

I appreciated the keen insight the Lord had given this man. Clearly, there is actually an increase in our evangelistic outreach.

The World Congress on Evangelism—organized, promoted and sponsored by the Billy Graham Organization in conjunction with Carl Henry, Editor of Christianity Today—was probably one of the most significant conferences since the days of the apostles. It was Billy's personal wish that I attend this magnificent conference, and I'm glad I did, for it was one of the greatest experiences of my life.

HARVEST OF HEALING

During the past few months the Lord has been dealing with me. I have been seeking His direction for our future ministry. I have known generally that I was to seek the lost and bring healing to humanity — healing for the whole person, body, mind and soul. Healing is the soul being cleansed from sin and made right with God; the mind, freed from fear, conflicts and anxiety; the body, delivered from sickness and disease. I knew this was my command. I knew, too, I needed further guidance from God in order to fulfill it.

Usually the Lord speaks to me when I am alone. His voice comes quickly and then it is gone. This time, He spoke over an eight-day period. This experience began in the Norfolk Crusade, just before we left for Brazil. While Evelyn and I were eating dinner in our motel one evening, the Lord spoke to me. Immediately, I went to my room and started writing down everything He said. The moment I tried to understand, I lost contact. I told myself, *Don't let your intellect become the origin for this.* I didn't receive the entire message until Thursday night. Suddenly, the Lord spoke again. I quickly picked up a pencil and paper and wrote. This is what God said:

GOD'S MESSAGE

"I have given you 20 years of taking My healing power to your generation. Now in the rest of the time that I shall give you, I want you to take it even to the remotest bounds of the earth; not only you but those who are with you, those I have raised up to support and help you.

"Behold, I shall enlarge your borders and extend your hand to the millions — in a harvest of healing where you will seek the lost and suffering. You will go where they are, even to remote areas where My light is dim, My voice is heard small, and where My healing power is not known.

"You must find a way to enter into all nations, and I say all nations, with My word of healing. You must divide your work and time in America with the world — this is to be a mighty spreading and gathering.

"You shall suffer much for My glory. You have not been ready for this, but you are ready now. Work with the young; work with the old; work with everyone I shall send you to — especially raise up your students to hear My voice and to go to the uttermost parts of the earth. Their work will exceed yours and in this I am pleased. In their success, your ministry will rise to the heights you have always dreamed of. There is much reward ahead but there is much, much more to be done before the reward comes.

"You shall not be afraid to obey Me. Be not alarmed; be not afraid. This is your hour to move forward with your helpers to penetrate the hearts of the millions with My Gospel. Turn neither to the right hand nor to the left. Be reliable. Be courageous, always expecting Me to do miracles among the people. Millions are waiting for you; go to them.

"Again I say, do not be alarmed, I will brighten your way. The people will understand that I am sending you, that I am speaking, that I am working, that I am sending you as My very own chosen vessel. There is no power on earth that can stop you or even hinder you until I say, 'This work is done and this harvest is gathered.'"

TEAM

Through the years God has blessed me with a wonderful team. They are men who know how to get the job done and who can think on their feet. Best of all, they know Jesus and are led by the Holy Spirit. We've been in some tight spots together. We've been in places where we have nearly lost our lives. But through it all we have stood as a team. I thank God for each of them. Here are statements from some of my team members.

Since I came to work for Brother Roberts in September 1949, my life has become more meaningful and blessed of the Lord. During this time the influence of this ministry has grown until it has blessed people in all parts of the world. The Oral Roberts radio broadcast has become a vital force in reaching the world for Christ. All of us who have had a personal part in the broadcast have been singularly blessed by it. I thank God for this opportunity of service for Him.

— *G. Manford Engel, Vice-President of Development*

There were several things about this ministry that attracted me to it and changed my life. First, it has a spiritual anointing upon it that makes it very powerful. Second, it has an approach to truth that not only gives the wonderful blessing of God's presence in the meetings at the moment, but you also feel that you are getting something to live by, something that will help you meet tomorrow's problems and to face up to the responsibilities of life as there are needs. And third, there is an enthusiasm. It is an enthusiasm that challenges a person to reach new spiritual heights that they have not attained before.

— *Rev. R. F. DeWeese, Crusade Manager and Associate Evangelist*

Oral Roberts' ministry meets the needs of people. That may be an unsophisticated statement about a ministry that is in its twentieth year and reaches around the world...but it is a most important one. Just ask the millions who have been won to Christ and healed. This ministry leaps over preconceived notions about religion. It sheds the straitjacket of tradition. It is uncomplicated. It is direct. It goes straight to people's needs and confronts those needs with God's unlimited power and supply. Thanks be to God for all He has done through this ministry.

— *Al Bush, Executive Vice-President OREA*

Brother Roberts said to me recently, "Lee, the same God and Holy Spirit who called me into this deliverance ministry has also called me to build this University." I believe this with all my heart. I have been associated with Brother Roberts almost from the beginning of his deliverance ministry, and I have watched each new outreach come into being. I am excited about the outreach of the University. I see it as a bridge to bring together God's people of different backgrounds to be Christ's witnesses throughout the world.

— S. L. Braxton, Chairman, ORU Board of Regents

I have been terrifically impressed with President Roberts' burning desire to have the entire University deeply rooted in the love of Jesus Christ. To me, the high point of his years of ministry is the outreach of the University because of its many-faceted program. This includes the seminars. Thousands of people visit the campus with one objective in mind — that of deepening their spiritual relationship with the Lord. Here they are impelled to become firebrands and return to their various vocations and professions to minister to others.

— Dr. J. D. Messick, Executive Vice-President and Provost, ORU

I saw Oral Roberts for the first time when I attended the Tallahassee Crusade in 1949. It was a great thrill to see souls saved and people healed on such a gigantic scale. I realized that here was a man doing the work the church should be doing, and I felt that God had raised Oral Roberts up to do it. In the 16 years I have been associated with this ministry; it has challenged me to do more than I could do, and to be more than I could have been.

— Collins Steele, Crusade Equipment Manager

I see the Oral Roberts University as an extension of the ministry of the partners. Partners of this ministry have caught a vision of the work of the kingdom of God. They give as unto the Lord. Our graduates — who will not only be trained academically, but also have a deep understanding of the whole man, the way of deliverance — will reflect something of the sacrificial giving of every partner. As they go into every walk of life, they will be literally "going into all the world." They are the partners' personal outreach to all the world.

— Tommy Tyson, University Minister, ORU

How proud can one father, father-in-law and grandfather be? I'm all these rolled into one happy man. Left to right are my son and his wife, Ronnie and Carol; my son and daughter, Richard and Roberta; myself, Evelyn, and my son-in-law and daughter, Marshall and Rebecca Nash; and the pride of our lives, Brenda Ann Nash.

Brenda Ann Nash, our only grandchild, is our pride and joy. Evelyn decided one day that our grandchildren were going to call us "grandmother" and "grandfather." So from the time Brenda Ann started to try to talk she drilled her on "grandmother" and "grandfather." Brenda's first try came out: Danmana. Finally she dropped the "dan" and it has been Mana ever since. Then she attempted granddaddy. This was just too much. She opened her mouth and out came Andy. One day we were babysitting with her and I said, "Evelyn, do you suppose when this child is grown that she will call us Grandmother and Granddaddy?" I didn't think about Brenda's listening to us, but she looked up bright as a dollar and said, "No, it will always be Andy and Mana." When her mother and father take her riding by ORU, she will say, "Dere's Andy's university." I love to hear her talk, but I'm reminded daily that this is not my university — it is God's. It may always be "Andy's university" to Brenda, but one day she will know in her heart that it belongs to God.

In my leisure moments — which are few — I enjoy a game of golf.

Our son, Ronald David, was married March 5, 1966, to Carol Croskery and we have welcomed Carol into our family with open arms.

The Abundant Life Mural, located in the Prayer Tower, was unveiled June 9, 1960. The huge work of art, which took two years to complete, depicts the Abundant Life Concept through brilliant color, fluted glass, sculptured hands, with changing light and sound. The late Warren Straton, the artist who created the mural, said he felt it was one of his most outstanding works.

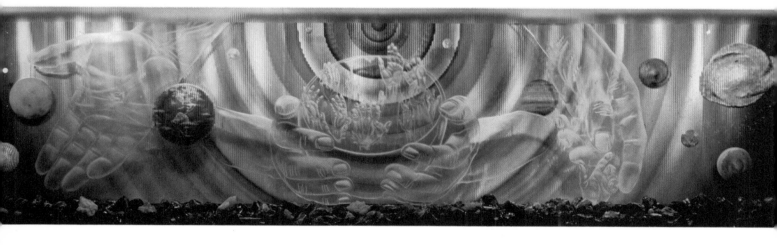

We Accept God's Challenge

We do not know if God will give us one year, five or twenty. But, whatever time He allots us will be spent with our team, our partners and our students, taking God's healing power to this generation.

During the Berlin World Congress on Evangelism last October, the delegates were unanimous in their cry, "Send us evangelists, teachers and others. Give us trained young people who are filled with the Spirit; then we can move our countries toward God."

We are ready to answer the call of God, to help meet the challenge of the hour while there is still time. We will go to lost and suffering humanity, whether they be in the by-ways of America or in distant lands. We will go even to remote areas where God's light is dim, where His voice is heard small and where His healing power is not known. We will move forward with God and reap a harvest of healing. That is why we pray that God will continue to give us clear direction, His anointing, and partners who feel what we feel for the lost and suffering of this generation.

A night view of the University that faith in God built.